CHRISTIANS

IN

CONFLICT

CHRISTIANS

IN

CONFLICT

EVERETT LEADINGHAM, EDITOR

Though this book is designed for group study, it is also intended
for personal enjoyment and spiritual growth. A leader's guide
is available from your local bookstore or your publisher.

Beacon Hill Press of Kansas City
Kansas City, Missouri

Copyright 2004
By Beacon Hill Press of Kansas City

ISBN: 083-412-0550

Printed in the United States of America

Editor: Everett Leadingham
Associate Editor: Charlie L. Yourdon
Executive Editor: Merritt Nielson

Cover Design: Paul Franitza
Cover Art: Corbis

10   9   8   7   6   5   4   3   2

CONTENTS

CHAPTER 1

CONFLICT IS EVERYWHERE

by DAVID W. HOLDREN

I WILL NEVER FORGET my conversation with Mary. It happened about five or six years into my pastoral career. I was asked to visit this lady who had been a faithful and involved church member for many years, but had mysteriously dropped out—and stayed out. I determined to find out why and help her with re-entry. As far as I know, I failed.

It was not my first visit with Mary, but it would turn out to be a pivotal one, perhaps more for me than her. After exchanging pleasantries, I decided to probe the issue of her abandonment of the church. In the end, she didn't reveal all the details. Rather, she confirmed that during a church remodeling project, a considerable storm had developed over, in her words, "a gallon of paint."

In retrospect, she may have told me more than I heard, but after her revelation about the heart of the storm, I heard little else for a few moments. Then I tried my best to address the issues of human stubbornness, bitterness, and the power of forgiveness. "Why let another retain such power over you?" I said. "Who wants to miss heaven over a gallon of paint?" You may challenge my theological framework, but I was astonished—a gallon of paint!

Does it seem that sometimes the casualties of conflict are greater than the cause for the conflict? Nevertheless, we know that everywhere we turn, conflict can be found—or it finds us.

What Is Conflict?

Simply put, conflict is *differences colliding*. The nature and damage of the collision depend on a lot of things, and that's where the Bible speaks to us in a host of healthy ways. You will be reading about them throughout this book.

The biblical writer James has a startling perspective on interpersonal conflict. In essence, he says that such conflict is a result of conflicting desires *within* us. These desires erupt into quarrels and clashes when we do not get what we want or want what others have. We will do about anything to have it or take it. Selfish motives dominate—and they destroy (see James 4:1-3).

Ironically, what we *really* need could have been better supplied through *prayer.*

Conflict occurs in courtrooms and classrooms and bedrooms. Our differences collide over theology, philosophy, psychology, and personality. We feud over issues of race, religion, and even recreation.

There is conflict in the animal kingdom, the human kingdom, and even the cosmos itself. Conflict is raging, at any given moment, on the ground, in the air, under ground, and beneath the sea, in some form or another. Our struggles are within and between. Conflict is a daily event, whether in community schoolyard scrapes or corporate skyscrapers. It happens at Madison Square Garden, over lawns and gardens, and even in the Garden of Eden.

The fact is, conflict can occur even in a perfect world. The Bible describes that early abode of Adam and Eve. The serpent first created a mental conflict about God by planting seeds of doubt in Eve's mind. Those seeds grew and led to choices of behavior that were disobedient to God's command. When God confronted them, everyone began blaming each other for what had happened. Adam and Eve probably had some additional, private words for each other that didn't get recorded in the Bible.

The discipline for their actions was a more conflicted relationship with the serpent and even nature itself. Before long, even the first siblings became rivals, and one killed the other. Things got worse, much worse. It finally caught up with humanity in the form of a cleansing flood (see Genesis 6).

Our story since then has been continual conflict. The history of civilization reveals that it hasn't been a very civil history. Unfortunately, even the history of Christianity has been littered with enough rivalry, bigotry, and even brutality to cause the most faithful to groan and wonder why.

In light of all the tensions that exist, one of the reasons for a reflective visit to a cemetery is to recall that all arguments are eventually laid to rest.

Levels of Conflict

Conflict has many faces, natures, and levels. Some parts are quite harmless and a normal part of problem-solving. Other aspects can become devastating. Let's look at brief descriptions of four levels of conflict.

1. *Problem-solving* is a mild level of conflict, where we compare and contrast ideas or methods, such as corporate strategies or selecting a college to attend. This level engages discussion and seeks solutions. It can get a bit heated, but ideally remains pretty calm.

2. *Disagreement* may lead from the first level. Many underlying reasons bring us into disagreement, such as differences in temperament, traditions, family background, perspective, underlying agendas, or expectations. Debate and tension are common at this level, and emotions may flare.

Often, as disagreement becomes more intense, those involved are tempted to build superhighways that take them from basic disagreement to all-out conflict. Some of these fast roads are sarcasm, personal insults, character attacks, exaggerated accusations of blame, and so on. These are some of the conflict dangers in marriage, as well as in other forums of life.

3. *Contest* is the level of conflict where it seems that the objective becomes winning at any cost. Tactics become more unpleasant. The original issue and its solution fade in importance and *winning* becomes the only goal. Usually, all parties lose.

4. *Relational warfare* is the most unfortunate degree of conflict. At this level, deep divisions occur as insults fly and the attacks become more brutal—even to the point of injury in some way (such as, damaging a reputation or inflicting emotional abuse). All manner of heartache and destruction occur as a result of this kind of warfare.

If we are aware of these various levels, it helps us to know what is normal, what to expect, and how to avoid escalation of conflict. Resolution is always easier at the earlier levels, before major devastation occurs. When we sense the tension rising, we need to take appropriate action without delay.

Conflict's Positive Side

Conflict is an invitation to discover win-win solutions. It offers a chance to clarify our expectations, uncover our assumptions, and bring light to misunderstandings. Conflict should prod us to evaluate situations, relationships, and even our personal motives and attitudes. It is a terrific opportunity for reconciliation and renewal. For sure, it tends to energize some people and depress others. Yet, hopefully, it gets us off dead center and opens up dialogue. It can spark creativity, and bring people together to pray and counsel and console.

Amazingly, it can be a pathway to *holiness!* The context of Matthew 5:48, regarding being complete (perfect) like our Heavenly Father, is the context of *love,* and further, loving our *enemies!*

Four Responses to Conflict

What can we learn from Christ and the Bible about dealing with conflict? There are four basic responses to conflict: avoid it, resolve it, manage it, or yield to it.

1. *Avoid it.* Of course, there are the more popular, though less honorable ways to avoid conflict, such as the "I don't want to get involved" excuse. Sometimes that line is valid, but often it is a reflection of failure to care enough or a failure of courage.

It helps to avoid conflict if you can *anticipate it.* As a fighter once said, "It is the punch that you don't see coming that knocks you out."

The half-brother of Jesus reminds us, "We all stumble in many ways. If anyone is never at fault in what he says, he is a perfect man" (James 3:2). The context of that verse is the use of the tongue, and the amazing "forest fires" that we can set with it. He is essentially telling us that in many ways we all offend. Therefore, learn to expect it, and plan how to avoid conflict or minimize the potential of offenses committed.

Over the years, this verse has taught me to build a "bumper zone" around everyone. In other words, I assume that sooner or later most anyone I know will do or say something that offends me. That is, they will "bump" into me. So I am not shocked when it happens and try not to react inappropriately. I attempt to be prepared to handle things with grace and care to preserve the relationship. Only recently, much to my chagrin, it became evident that others, too, have a "bumper zone" around me. Words I spoke were misquoted to others, and offense set in. On my part, silence would have been the better route in the first place.

It is probably true that the massive volume of opinions, judgments, criticisms, sarcasms, and those "don't tell anyone, but . . ." statements that we utter daily cause plenty of conflict and damaged relationships in our worlds.

Jesus admonished, "Do not judge, or you too will be judged" (Matthew 7:1). In one of the most convicting statements in Scripture, Jesus warned that we will give account for every careless word we speak. "I tell you that men will have to give account on the day of judgment for every careless word they have spoken. For by your words you will be acquitted, and by your words you will be condemned" (Matthew 12:36-37).

Possibly the best written advice regarding the tongue and avoiding conflict is, "Do not let any *unwholesome talk* come out of your mouths, but only what is helpful for building others up according to their needs, that it may benefit those who listen" (Ephesians 4:29, emphasis added).

That is how we avoid a lot of conflict in life, and how we build powerful and lasting relationships!

Avoiding conflict, however, is not the highest value we are discussing in this chapter. Even Jesus, on numerous occasions, *invited* conflict. Even a casual reading of the Gospels will reveal that He said and did things against the religious sensitivities of His day that He knew would incite criticism and wrath. So, too, there are those times in life when we believe that the cause is worth it, and choose to speak or act with purpose and awareness of the reactions and consequences.

We are wise to understand human nature and the specific tendencies and patterns of the folks we relate to on a regular basis. On the basis of our knowledge, we can prepare how to react and respond when something is said or done that otherwise would lead to conflict if we had not anticipated it.

The apostle Paul gave us a sound example when he said, "I have fought the good fight" (2 Timothy 4:7). That line has many lessons in it, but one of them is *choose our fights.* Many hassles in life are not "good" fights; they are not worth it. So, avoid them. Save energy for worthy engagements and causes.

The writer of Proverbs gave us good counsel when he advised that a gentle answer deflects wrath (see Proverbs 15:1).

2. *Resolve it.* This is the best-case scenario, once conflict has become a reality. Resolving conflict is the discovery of a solution for the conflict and those embroiled in it. The instruction Jesus gave His disciples on prayer was brief, yet had a focus on resolution: "Forgive us our debts, as we also have forgiven our debtors" (Matthew 6:12).

One of the most powerful and effective lessons my wife
and I have learned about resolving conflict is to distinguish
between the *issues* of conflict and the *injuries* of conflict.
They are two very different things. We desperately need to
realize that *we can live with differences, but we can't live well
with the damage they can cause.*

Once again, it is the Word that instructs us. One brief
verse in Ephesians says it so well. "'In your anger do not sin':
Do not let the sun go down while you are still angry" (4:26).
Wow! Let's take a look at what is packed into this dynamite
statement.

First, it takes Christians off the hook (a little) about anger, by assuming that it occurs. Then, it challenges us about
what we do with our anger ("Do not sin"). It is not the emotion of anger itself that is wrong, but what we do with it de-
termines what it becomes. So, in times of conflict, this verse
is telling us we must deal with the volatile emotion of anger
and hostile feelings.

"But," you may say, "what about when we get into a difference of opinion that escalates into an argument, and it is
time to turn out the lights and go home, yet the conflict is
not resolved?" Great question, and a very common dilemma.

Most people assume that we should just "sleep on it"
and it will go away. Wrong! Suppressed anger and conflict
have a way of showing up later in a variety of forms. The
tensions simmer, and unresolved emotional conflict can
lead to resentment, which can inflict long-term damage on
relationships.

So, what kind of hint is in this verse that resolution is
needed? The words about not letting the sun set while we
are still angry is the word of admonition to reconcile. "But,"
you might be thinking, "what if the disagreement is real and
unresolved?" Good question. However, God's Word is addressing the *emotion* (anger), not the *issue.*

This insightful instruction calls for us to resolve the emotional separation and damage, whether or not the issue is

still under debate. The fact is, humans can get along with many differences of opinion, as long as we keep resolving the feelings that can come between us. This happens as one party has the grace and courage to confess his or her part in the tension and ask forgiveness. If all parties involved do the same, resolution can occur, and everyone can live to dialogue another day.

In a brilliant insight on the purpose and power of worship, Jesus told us that if we are in the midst of worship and realize we have offended another, we should leave and resolve the issue—as a continuing act of our worship (see Matthew 5:23-24).

Another set of activities that leads to resolution is summarized by using the words "resolve conflict" as an acrostic:

Recognize the need
Engage in dialogue
Stick with the issue
Overlook sidetracking tendencies
Learn to love, even during conflict
View the issue from the other's perspective
Explore options

Clarify the issues
Open your mind
Never say "never" or "always"
Focus on core issues
Listen for feelings
Imagine yourself in the other's place
Compromise can be win-win
Timing is vital

3. *Manage it.* There are times when the essence of the conflict continues. In those situations, the negative consequences can be minimized if the conflict is managed well and wisely.

Legal systems use mediators for corporate clashes, marriage problems, and a host of conflict issues. Towns and cities appoint mediating teams to address escalating issues that have potential for increasing hostility. Negotiators are involved in everything from hostage situations to sports contracts. All are intending to serve, literally, as agents of conflict management and resolution.

Conflict is best managed when people on differing sides *agree to some guidelines and ground rules* for addressing the dispute. Such guidelines may be:

- Stick to the issue
- No character attacks
- Own your feelings, rather than blame others for them
- Avoid building highways that lead to hostilities

Conflict is better managed as involved parties work to discover the issues, keeping in mind that the surface issue is not always the most significant issue.

The words and behaviors given to us in Ephesians 4:25-32 are an absolute treasure of wisdom for not only managing, but avoiding and resolving conflict. As we take time to read and ponder these verses, we can identify and reflect on the various parts of the counsel given, and even ask God's Spirit to help us with ones that fit present needs.

The entirety of Matthew 5, which is a portion of Jesus' words that we refer to as the Sermon on the Mount, is loaded with wisdom that can help us avoid, and even transform conflict.

4. *Yield to it.* This may sound like a strange response to conflict, but it has its own value and power. Jesus referred to a form of such yielding when He told us that we are blessed when we are reviled and misused for God's sake. He said to rejoice and be glad because of the reward that awaits us, and that we are neither the first nor the last who suffer for the faith (see Matthew 5:11-12).

A bit later in the same sermon, Jesus said that there is a time to *not resist* one who abuses us for the faith (see vv. 38-42). Absorb the abuse and come back for more, as it were. Before this is misunderstood, let me hasten to add that the context of these statements is persecution for our *faith*. This is not addressing a marriage or parenting situation nor criminal acts or nations attacking nations.

The ultimate example of yielding to conflict is Jesus Christ and His death on the Cross. Could He have avoided it? We believe so. Could He have counterattacked? Certainly, but He did not. His follower Peter had lucid recollections of Jesus yielding to the attacks on His honor and life. About those memories, he said, "When they hurled their insults at him, he did not retaliate; when he suffered, he made no threats. Instead, he entrusted himself to him who judges justly" (1 Peter 2:23). Peter prefaced this revelation by admonishing us to "follow in [Christ's] steps" (v. 21).

Conflict *Is* Everywhere

In summary, conflict is all around us, and often within us. Paul wrote to the Christians at Rome, "If it is possible, as far as it depends on you, live at peace with everyone" (Romans 12:18). That is essentially the Christian creed as it relates to conflict and peace. However, as the verse recognizes, it is not always possible to avoid it. So, we must *recognize our personal responsibility*, to avoid conflict when possible and to address it when it arises. And we must exercise grace to help *resolve emotional conflict*, even though differences exist. Through confession, forgiveness, and discovery of solution, we must reconcile when possible.

Actually, it is a wonderful thing to realize that the essence of the gospel is about bringing ultimate solution to irresolvable conflict, through the grace of God as well as the intercession and reconciliation made possible by Christ. As the apostle Paul said, "God, who reconciled us to himself through Christ and gave us the ministry of reconciliation . . . has committed to us the message of reconciliation" (2 Corinthians 5:18-19).

Fight the good fight, finish the course, and keep the faith!

Scriptures Cited: Genesis 6; Proverbs 15:1; Matthew 5:11-12, 23-24, 38-42; 6:12; 7:1; 12:36-37; Romans 12:18; 2 Corinthians 5:18-19; Ephesians 4:25-32; 2 Timothy 4:7; James 3:2; 4:1-3; 1 Peter 2:21, 23

About the Author: Dr. David Holdren is a general superintendent of The Wesleyan Church.

CHAPTER 2

CLASHING WITH STRANGERS

by MARTHA VANCISE

CHRIS, ALREADY LATE for an appointment, was stuck behind a slow-moving vehicle in the fast lane. The car ahead of him maintained the same speed as an adjacent vehicle in the slow lane. Side by side, the vehicles traveled, blocking Chris's route. After a mile, Chris impatiently tapped the horn. Without as much as a glance in the rearview mirror, the driver continued at the same pace. The driver's attention seemed focused on a new housing development on the other side of the road rather than on the traffic.

Another mile passed. Chris moved close to the rear bumper of the car ahead and held the horn down. Finally, the driver glanced into the mirror and moved into the slow lane. Chris floored the accelerator, and as he passed the slower vehicle, he gave the driver a hard stare. When Chris saw the driver's face, he groaned. The driver was a neighbor who had retired and recently moved into Chris's neighborhood. Chris had been trying to get him to attend a home Bible study.

When asked to relate an incident of conflict with strangers, we often reply with a similar driving story. We joke about conflict on the highway and readily admit that we clash with strangers when we drive. We have problems with strangers in other places also, but we tend to vent our anger more readily in traffic situations. Why? Although in recent years, people have been shot in road rage incidents, we usually feel that our vehicle will protect us from the other person's response. In the safety of our cars, we use the horn, drive too close, scowl, and even mouth our outrage. If we were in direct contact with the person outside of our vehicles, we would probably temper our response.

Why Can't We Get Along?

Without hesitation, we entertain our friends with these embellished traffic stories, but few of us readily admit to conflict with strangers in other situations. Each day, though, we deal with many people we don't know, and we often express frustration by our attitudes, words, and actions. We encounter strangers in checkout lines, waiting rooms, medical facilities, schools, colleges, restaurants, stadiums, at work, and in places of recreation. We even let unknown persons into our homes when we open the door to service personnel or answer the call of a telemarketer. Why do we have clashes with strangers? These people are only passing through our lives for a few moments, or at the most a few hours. Why can't we graciously interact with them?

Because strangers create anxiety for us. Since childhood, we have been taught to be wary of strangers. Survival requires that we pass on this wariness to our children. As we mature, though, we realize that few people intend to harm us, so we usually ignore unknown persons unless we have reason to interact with them.

When our paths unavoidably intersect with strangers, we often sense anxiety. In some places, this anxiety may include fear of being physically harmed, such as being robbed and beaten. More often, though, it includes anxiety over losing control of what we value in our lives: pleasure, use of our time, leadership roles, self-esteem, friendships, family relationships, and even ways of worship. While strangers can threaten almost any aspect of our lives, we most often come into direct conflict in areas relating to our children, time, space, or authority.

Children

Protection of our young is a basic, God-given instinct. Even a mother hen will enfold her chicks under her wings and fight an intruder. At some time during child-rearing years, parents will find themselves in conflict with their child's friends, parents of friends, or teachers. Most of these conflicts are transitory and can be resolved in a teacher's conference or over a neighborly cup of coffee.

A more serious type of conflict arises when strangers teach our children values that run counter to Christian principles. Neighborhood, school, TV, radio, and sometimes even church no longer are automatically safe havens. On every side, other people hand our children variant views of acceptable behavior. As parents in an increasingly secular world, we must take time to meet the strangers who daily influence our children. Protection of our children may require confronting these persons.

Time

In many cultures, arriving two hours later than an appointed time is acceptable. In our culture, we will violate speed limits and cut conversations short in order to get to an appointment on time. We say, "Time is money," and we guard it as if it really were currency. This doesn't mean that we always spend our time wisely; it means that we want to be in charge of spending it. When a stranger reaches into our life and pulls out a handful of our time, conflict often arises. We may spend an hour watching trivia about a TV star that we'll never meet, but fret over losing two minutes to an elderly lady who is laboriously counting out pennies for exact change.

How do we express our conflict? Do we curse or make obscene gestures? Never! We're Christians. Rather, we mutter under our breath, sigh loudly, and roll our eyes at those around us. However, are those passive-aggressive actions much different in their attitude?

Space

Along with protecting our time, we jealously guard our space. This space includes physical distance from other bodies, and all the sights, sounds, and even smells that enter our space. Conflict comes when an uninvited stranger's perfume, body odor, music, or conversation enters our personal space. Our protected space includes our entire airline seat—even the tray on the back of our seat that a six-year-old repeatedly slams into place. Conflict with strangers comes when their raucous celebration in a restaurant disturbs the quiet of our long-anticipated candlelight dinner.

Authority

Invasion of our time and space creates most of our conflict with strangers. Even when we have conflict with those in authority, the basic concern is usually over their invading our privacy or squandering our time. As more laws and security measures take effect in our world, persons in authority increasingly affect us. When we enter gated communities, businesses, government offices, schools, and airports, we must yield to questions, searches, and even temporary confiscation of some possessions. Strangers enter our place of business and probe, check, and report on whether we are adhering to county, state, and federal laws.

When these probers are novices, they sometimes misuse their newly gained authority and delay us unnecessarily. Those who travel, especially in foreign countries, watch time sift through the hands of strangers who must dot every legal "i" and cross every "t" to make sure that we know who is in charge and controls our actions for the moment.

Everywhere we go, we are going to find strangers who irritate us and give us reasons to clash with them.

I Touched You Last!

These arguments probably started with children in the backseat of a donkey-drawn cart. No matter what starts a backseat conflict, the issue soon becomes who touched last. In airports, theme parks, church, and shopping malls, strangers sometimes stray into our personal space and brush us in a way that irritates us. They demand immediate attention from a salesperson while we wait our turn. They drive in the emergency lane in order to merge with traffic ahead of us. The boom of their audio system drowns the nature sounds we enjoy in the evening. Anger flares over their intrusion into our space, and their shoving aside of our rights. Conflict, however, will not arise unless we "touch back."

When a stranger's actions make us want to "touch back," we might ask ourselves some questions.

Do I need to respond to this?

In the majority of cases, we do not need to respond to conflict with strangers. Conflict will not occur until we return the "touch" or respond to the stranger. As long as "touching" continues, conflict will continue. When Chris was behind the slow vehicle, was it necessary for him to tailgate the slow car and blow the horn a long time? Not really. We seldom need to respond to a stranger's irritating ways.

Does this involve safety?

On rare occasions, we must enter conflict with strangers to preserve our lives and to protect those we love. Had Chris been on his way to the hospital with a wife in labor, saving two lives would have been a factor in his response. In situations involving safety, we must respond immediately and may even need to call for help from law enforcement. The response to danger will differ from a response to inconvenience.

What difference will it make a hundred years from now?

We often say, "Don't sweat the small stuff." We would do well to ask how much difference our immediate actions will make in the long run. Many of our encounters with strangers will end within a few minutes or, at most, a few hours. Occasionally, the situation can have long-term effects. A teacher who scoffs at God as the Creator can eternally influence our child's attitude toward biblical doctrines. In some situations, we must act to prevent dangerous, perhaps permanent, consequences.

Can the person with whom I'm in conflict make any needed change?

Understaffing puts workers at risk for conflict with those they serve. Many of these employees are already stressed. If we add to their stress, will it enable them to work faster and meet our needs sooner? When action is necessary, go to the person who can actually improve the situation.

Is this my business? Am I the person who should take action?

We are familiar with the heroic efforts of Todd Beamer and other passengers when they made it their business to act against the strangers who controlled their flight on September 11, 2001. While we hope that we will never face a similar decision, we do encounter other issues that result in conflict with strangers. Should we enter conflict with strangers who sell drugs in our neighborhood? What should we do about the stranger whose children always have bruises and appear malnourished? Doing the right thing may involve life-threatening conflict with strangers.

Oops!!

More often than we realize, we irritate strangers. Just like the slow driver ahead of Chris, we aren't paying attention to the task at hand. We're enjoying life in our own little space, oblivious to our encroachment on another's space or time. The honking horn, the scowl, the harsh remarks are sometimes directed at us. We've "touched" a stranger; he or she has "touched back." The old backseat question quickly surfaces, "Who touched last?" In these brief encounters with strangers, defense of our actions seldom helps. Let it go. Refuse to "touch back."

Even Jesus encountered conflict. People (who may or may not have been strangers to Him) continually approached, trying to start arguments. How did He handle such encounters? Jesus often turned the dispute into a spiritual lesson. When religious leaders tried to trap Jesus with questions about the adulterous woman, He turned their contention into a lesson on forgiveness (see John 8:1-11). He turned discord over Sabbath observance into a lesson on mercy (see Luke 6:1-9). He told His followers that when strangers compelled them to go a mile, they should give them two miles of time and energy (see Matthew 5:41).

Paul continually had conflict with strangers. The Jews in Damascus plotted to kill him (see Acts 9:23); both Gentiles and Jews planned to stone him in Iconium (see 14:5). When Paul tells of his sufferings at the hand of strangers, he begins the litany by saying, "We put no stumbling block in anyone's path, so that our ministry will not be discredited" (2 Corinthians 6:3). Paul knew that although strangers had beaten him, told falsehoods, plotted to kill him, and imprisoned him, his manner of handling conflict would have long-term effects on his ministry. When we have conflict with strangers, our response will not only affect those with whom we have conflict, but will influence those who observe our conflict. Those observers often include our children.

Paul viewed contact with strangers as opportunities to point people to Christ. He told the Colossians, "Be wise in the way you act toward outsiders; make the most of every opportunity" (Colossians 4:5).

On Sunday mornings, we sing and pray, "Lord, lead me to some needy soul today." On Monday, when God puts strangers so squarely on our path that we stumble over them, we complain about how they messed up our weekly planner. All week long we brush aside scores of opportunities to show kindness to strangers as we travel, work, or shop; but on Sunday morning, we rush to shake the hand of one visitor who walks into our church. Kind responses during the week will produce more Christians than mere handshakes at church.

Sometimes seizing an opportunity to do good may mean that we must give up some of our rights. Paul told us to have the same attitude as Christ, who did not hold onto His rights as God, but became a man, a servant, subject to a humiliating death in order to give us eternal life (see Philippians 2:5-8).

To be certain, some strangers take away our rights. We have the right to the handicapped-parking spot, fair value for our money, the seat on a crowded bus, safety to walk our dog through the park. When strangers have offended us or invaded our personal space, we often want to make sure that "they know that we know" our rights have been violated. We want to sling that scowl or growl back at them. Paul told the Christians at Rome, "Do not repay anyone evil for evil. Be careful to do what is right in the eyes of everybody. If it is possible, as far as it depends on you, live at peace with everyone" (Romans 12:17). These minor conflicts can provide opportunities to preserve our rights (but at what expense?) or to present a Christlike witness. We have the choice.

Make My Day

Conflict with strangers *will* happen. We can handle conflict with strangers in three ways.

1. We can "touch back" (that is, defend our position).
2. We can ignore or walk away from the situation.
3. We can turn the conflict into a positive encounter.

Occasionally, events happen so quickly that we react to protect others and ourselves. These incidents often involve danger. For the most part, though, we have time to evaluate a situation and choose a response. James told us to be "quick to listen, slow to speak and slow to become angry" (1:19).

Sometimes walking away is our best option. When the people at Nazareth grew unruly, Jesus slipped through the crowd and vanished (see Luke 4:14-30). Paul went out a window in a basket when strangers' plot to kill him was uncovered (see Acts 9:23-25). We don't expect to be climbing out of windows to avoid conflict, but we can turn and walk away. Whether a stranger started the conflict or we inadvertently caused it, sometimes we simply need to walk away.

There are times when removing our children from a negative influence may be our best option.

Conflict with strangers produces responses ranging from smiles to murder. In recent years, many Christians have responded to these conflicts with lawsuits. Sometimes legal action must be taken, but as Christians we would do well to carefully evaluate the conflict, consider the options of response, and follow Paul's advice to the Ephesians. "Be very careful, then, how you live—not as unwise but as wise, making the most of every opportunity, because the days are evil. Therefore do not be foolish, but understand what the Lord's will is" (5:15-17). Take time to know God's will. Before taking legal or continuing action against a stranger, ask yourself, "Is this an opportunity to lay aside my own rights to leave a strong Christian witness?"

Opportunities Galore

How do we seize the opportunity to leave a positive witness with strangers who irritate us? Sometimes a smile will work. The stranger may ignore us or even scowl at us, but we can walk away from every encounter knowing that we touched a stranger with the grace of kindness. Paul, who even suffered at the hands of persons in the church (did he know them all?), said, "Let us not become weary in doing good, for at the proper time we will reap a harvest if we do not give up. Therefore, as we have opportunity, let us do good to all people, especially to those who belong to the family of believers" (Galatians 6:9-10). Treating strangers with kindness not only keeps peace with them, but often produces a harvest of peace in our own hearts.

My friend Meribeth can attest to this truth. She rushed from one physician's office to another, delivering time-sensitive reports. As she left one office and hurried to her car, she stepped aside to allow a man to pass. She said, "Good morning," and smiled broadly at him. He continued without a response, and she walked on to her car.

"Miss!" she heard the man call. "Miss!"

She didn't have time to stop, but she paused and turned to see what he wanted.

"Miss," he said. "Thank you for that 'good morning' and your smile. It made my day."

It made her day too.

Scriptures Cited: Matthew 5:41; Luke 4:14-30; 6:1-9; John 8:1-11; Acts 9:23-25; 14:5; Romans 12:17; 2 Corinthians 6:3; Galatians 6:9-10; Ephesians 5:15-17; Philippians 2:5-8; Colossians 4:5; James 1:19

About the Author: Martha VanCise is a freelance author living in Ft. Pierce, Florida.

CHAPTER 3

ROOTS OF THE DISPUTES

by JACK M. BARNELL

FOR MANY YEARS I worked as a marriage and family therapist. By the time most couples made an appointment to see
me, they knew their marriage was unhealthy. Spouses usually offered different explanations for the sick condition of the
relationship, but often their sense of discomfort about the
marriage was because of serious and continual conflict.

I asked one couple to describe the issues that were trou-
bling their marriage. The husband said, "If she would just
do what I tell her, our marriage would be fine."

Another couple walked swiftly into my office with just a
terse greeting to me. Their faces were screwed into heavy
frowns. They looked at the floor. The husband blurted out,
"This is all so ridiculous. We can't even say 'good morning'
to each other without arguing!"

While I was sitting on a plane, the captain announced a
long delay in takeoff. The flight attendant began conversing
with me and discovered that I was a counseling therapist.
She said, "We are having problems with my husband's son."
Another attendant joined our conversation and said, "I
know what you mean. My husband's children are in conflict
with our children."

These instances indicate that conflict is common as we
relate to one another. Some words used to describe conflict
are "collision," "struggle," and "clash." Conflict may be described as *a disagreement that has become intense.*

Any time two people interact, they may engage in conflict.
Each has an opinion about the topic or the situation. Each

has an expectation about an appropriate response. Each is a unique personality. Each sees the world differently. How do these differences lead to conflict? What causes some of the conflicts that we experience in our relationships with others?

The Need for Power

People frequently have conflicts over power. As a couple entered my office, they continued an argument that they were having in the car. The wife was upset over the way her husband was spending their money. He had just bought something that cost over $200 without talking with her. She was severely upset about the impact this would have on their resources. She was angry. Since they had not discussed the purchase ahead of time, she felt ignored and insignificant in the marriage. She felt like she had no power to effect change in their lives. The husband seemed to be unaware of the reasons for the conflict.

Single adults can have conflicts with intrusive parents who want to be involved in the major decisions of their adult offspring. A young man spent several sessions with me, working through issues of his childhood. As he slowly came to the conclusion that he could redefine his parents' discipline in positive ways, he dismissed much of the anger he had felt toward them.

Then he decided to invite them to a session so he could set some boundaries with them for his young adulthood. With God's help, he was able to express appreciation for their concern for his welfare. He also was specific about his expectations for their interactions with him at this stage of life. His parents released him to follow his dreams, and he committed himself to future healthy interactions with them. They discovered how to share power in the relationship.

Adult children who return to the nest may have conflict with parents if boundaries are not defined at the outset. I met a couple whose adult son had recently moved back in with them. They were upset that he paid no money for anything and seemed to have no plans for leaving. I asked, "What agreements did you reach before he moved in about expenses, sharing of chores, and length of stay?" They answered, "We didn't talk about any of those things."

These parents set the stage for conflict because they didn't define expectations at the beginning of a new living arrangement. When their son failed to meet their unexpressed expectations, they felt like he was being disrespectful of them. As a result, they felt a loss of power in the relationship.

Some married couples conflict with their in-laws over who is in charge of the marriage relationship. A recently married couple came to me in distress because the man's parents were jealous of his closeness with his wife. The parents were concerned about losing power over their son now that he was married. They had the opportunity to relate to him as a peer instead of a dependent child, but they could only see their situation as a loss of power.

People may have conflicts about many issues with ex-spouses as they live out the reality of divorce. They often become involved in a power struggle. One divorced mother never had her children ready at the time agreed upon for their father to take them. She tried to make up for her feelings of powerlessness in the relationship by making her ex-husband wait. Another mother sent her children in soiled and ragged clothes to visit their father and his girlfriend in order to embarrass him. A divorced father told me that he often changed plans for returning the children just so he could get even with his ex-wife for not keeping her word. In these and other ways, people express their need for power.

When Jesus' disciples argued among themselves about who was the greatest, He called them aside and said, "If anyone wants to be first, he must be the very last, and the servant of all" (Mark 9:35). Part of the task of being Christian is learning that Christ is our source of power. When we fully acknowledge Him in that way, we become less concerned about our individual power in relationships.

The Need to Be Right

For many people, it is more important to be right than it is to find resolution for differences. One husband said to me, "I bring my check home and give it to my wife. I don't know where it all goes. I don't even get five dollars for spending money." I asked him how it helped for him to blame his wife for these circumstances, since he was the one who gave total control of finances to her. He seemed to be more interested in criticizing her for the situation than he was in owning his responsibility for changing it.

For many of us, the strong need to be right is a validation of self. We have been taught that we are less loved or less valued when we lose. We then connect value and love to being right. We learn to be right at any cost in order to try to avoid the pain of losing love and value. We fail to realize that, if the relationship wins, we all win. If one of us wins, the relationship loses.

James spoke to our need to be right when he wrote, "What causes fights and quarrels among you? Don't they come from your desires that battle within you? You want something but don't get it. You kill and covet, but you cannot have what you want. You quarrel and fight. You do not have, because you do not ask God. When you ask, you do not receive, because you ask with wrong motives, that you may spend what you get on your pleasures" (4:1-3). If we want to receive grace from God, we must submit to Him our need to be right.

The Need for Significance

Significance has to do with the way we think others perceive us. It answers the question, "How do others value me?"

We cause ourselves conflict and disappointment when we think that someone else is supposed to make us feel valuable. A mother was in tears as she sat in my office with her teenaged son. He was in trouble again with the law. She recounted the many ways she had rescued him from consequences in the past, but his behavior had not improved. She wailed, "I just wanted him to be happy." She tried to feel valuable by making her son dependent on her. She thought if she could avoid conflict with him and make his life smooth, he would love her and give her significance.

We aren't significant because someone else says it. We have significance because God values us. The apostle Paul said it this way, "While we were still sinners, Christ died for us" (Romans 5:8). We were His enemies, but Christ still loved us. We can't impress Him with our goodness. We can't do anything to make Him love us more or to love us less. He simply loves and validates us because we are His creation.

The Need for Meaning

Meaning has to do with the value we attach to ourselves. It answers the question, "How do I view myself?"

In our culture, we value those who work. When we meet a person, we may ask his or her name first, but the second question is often, "How do you make a living?" As a result, many people define themselves by their vocation. Some find it hard to retire because they think they have no meaning apart from their work.

We may experience conflict over expectations about employment. I counseled an unemployed young man who felt pressure from parents and friends to take a low-paying job until he found something better. He felt devalued by accepting a job that failed to challenge his strengths.

Couples may be in conflict over who works, what hours they work, and in what part of the country. Since most couples both work outside of the home, what happens when one gets a promotion that requires relocating to another area? If they don't discuss all aspects of the issue, they may set themselves up for repeated disagreements.

One couple talked with me about their conflicts on this

issue. To take a challenging career opportunity for the wife, they moved to another state. The husband left a job he liked and took a position with less pay and prestige. He battled continual depression because he defined his meaning by his position. He blamed his wife for his unhappiness.

Slowly this young man accepted the truth that he had meaning as a person, not a performer. He identified his meaning by his relationship to God. This freed him to find enjoyment in his work from a healthier perspective. He realized the fact that he was responsible for his moods and his outlook on life. When he chose to see God at work in his circumstances, he found new meaning in life. He came to understand Paul's words, "For it is God who works in you to will and to act according to his good purpose" (Philippians 2:13). When we recognize that God is at work in us, we may have fewer conflicts over our need for meaning.

The Need for Connection

We are relational people. We seek connection to others through many relationships, such as family, religion, friends, and recreation. Many of us dislike the feeling of being alone, and we often experience conflict as we try to meet our need for connection.

A wife sat in my office, crying about the disconnection she felt in her marriage. Her husband acted in ways that pushed her away from him. She said, "I'm tired of picking up his dirty clothes wherever he drops them." I asked her how she taught him to treat her this way, but she didn't know. How did he choose to be disrespectful of his wife? He may have learned it at home, but his wife chose to continue what his parents started. He was not held accountable. There were no consequences for his littering, and now at age 30 and with four children, he pursued his childish habit. His wife was parenting him, and the marriage was sick.

Some people find it difficult to move from singleness to being married. They want to be connected through marriage, but they still want to continue their weekly guys' or girls' night out. Other people who spend unusual amounts of time with video or computer games or in pursuit of personal fitness find that their connections with friends suffer. When we think about our behaviors, we should ask, "Does my participation in this behavior bring me closer to friends, family, or spouse, or does it drive them away from me? Could I still participate in this activity but less frequently?"

Paul's words to the Romans may help us here. He wrote, "Each of us will give an account of himself to God . . . Let us therefore make every effort to do what leads to peace and to mutual edification" (14:12, 19).

The Need to Preserve Self

The basic reason we experience conflict is that we are selfish, but there are times when conflict results from differing opinions about how to get a project done or in what direction to proceed. This conflict does not necessarily come from the self-centeredness of the participants. The Book of Acts notes such an event. Paul and Barnabas strongly disagreed about how to proceed with missionary work. Both were filled with God's Spirit, but they still experienced conflict. We read about how the conflict was resolved, "They had such a sharp disagreement that they parted company" (15:39).

Much of the time, however, we conflict with others because we want our own way. Paul described for the Romans the behavior of a self-centered person. "I have the desire to do what is good, but I cannot carry it out. For what I do is not the good I want to do; no, the evil I do not want to do— this I keep on doing" (7:18b-19).

A young husband eyed his feet miserably while his wife told me that he hurried to their computer each night without even greeting her after they had been separated all day. He could not wait to begin playing his games. She resented his addiction to the machine and his utter disregard for connecting with her. When I asked him how it helped the marriage for him to do this, he said, "It doesn't help, but I just need to 'veg out.'" He was doing what he wanted to do. We talked about ways that each spouse could meet individual needs while still nurturing their relationship.

We are born with the desire to preserve self. As we grow and discover our individuality, we develop a view of the world with self at the center. We interpret this concept of self to mean that others should bring us pleasure, should agree with us, and should embrace our view of the world. For most of us, the socialization process of childhood tempers this attitude. We learn to bend enough to get along with others. However, the basic selfish condition persists in our hearts and leads us to conflict with others about many matters simply because they behave differently from us.

After Paul described the self-centeredness mentioned in Romans 7, he concluded with these words, "What a wretched man I am! Who will rescue me from this body of death? Thanks be to God—through Jesus Christ our Lord!" (7:24-25). Thank God there is a way out from our selfishness.

Conclusion

When we confront another and seek to place blame or induce shame, we only increase the differences between us. People resent and resist blame. Shame induces self-doubt and depression. Blame does not bring about behavior change and growth. Shame does not bring new inner direction. However, if we confront people in order to stimulate responsibility, then we invite them to look at past behavior differently. We may then consider new behavior that can be more satisfying to both of us.

Responsibility focuses on the present. It is the ability to respond—"response" ability. When we take responsibility for the past, we affirm our ability to let God help us to respond in new ways to the present.

When we face conflict, we may ask the question, "Who is to blame?" Yet, the more important question is, "How can God and I respond to this conflict?" We can invite those in conflict to finish the past by dropping old demands and canceling old criticisms. If we step into moments of conflict in the spirit of Christ, we can help to bring healing. We can "care-front" others by being truthful and by owning our decisions and actions. We may pledge to risk behaving in new ways.

Who is to blame for conflict? It really doesn't matter. When we own the various causes of conflict, then we can decide in what ways to respond. We will resolve no conflict until we own our part in it. If we say, "It's all my fault," we see ourselves as more powerful than we are, because we are not the only players on the scene. If we say, "It's all your fault," we have denied our part in the situation. If we are honest, we will help each other own the issue and move toward resolution.

Paul provides us the key to dealing with the causes of conflict, "Love keeps no score of wrongs; does not gloat over other men's sins, but delights in the truth. There is nothing love cannot face; there is no limit to its faith, its hope, and its endurance" (1 Corinthians 13:5-7, NEB).

Scriptures Cited: Mark 9:35; Acts 15:39; Romans 5:8; 14:12, 19; 7:18b-19, 24-25; 1 Corinthians 13:5-7; Philippians 2:13; James 4:1-3

About the Author: Dr. Jack M. Barnell is a professor emeritus of MidAmerica Nazarene University, Olathe, Kansas.

CHAPTER 4

DISAGREEMENTS AT WORK

by EVERETT LEADINGHAM

WORK IS AN ESSENTIAL part of life. It consumes the lion's share of our time, day after day, week in and week out.

In fact, work consumes so much of our waking lives that we have specialized ways of talking about it. Most of the time when we meet someone new, as soon as we learn his or her name, we immediately ask, "What do you do?" What kind of work we do defines so much of who we are and how others perceive us.

We also have many old sayings about work. The farmers used to say, "There's always one more thing to do around the farm." Their wives put it this way, "A man works from sun to sun, but a woman's work is never done."

Regardless of how we describe work, or whether we enjoy work or not, all of us have our jobs to do. Some of us work in the home, not earning a paycheck but managing a household and rearing children. Others earn their money by working at home. Most wage-earners still leave the house and go to a particular place to work—be it a store, a factory, or an office.

Those who spend 40 or 60 or even 80 hours a week working outside the home have a special challenge—conflict in the workplace. In this chapter, we will look at that special challenge from three perspectives. First, are those problems we have with those who are over us in authority. Second, some of us have others who work for us, and we may have some difficulties there. Finally, a nearly universal experience for those who work away from home is conflict of one sort or another with coworkers.

A good place to start our discussion is with a man who had an unusual working environment. When Moses transferred from the Sheep and Goat division of tending the flock to the newly formed "Free the Slaves" project, he faced all the problems found in any current employment situation. Moses had disagreements with his "Boss," so to speak, on various occasions. He had problems with those he was trying to lead. And he had conflict with his "coworkers," in this case his brother and his sister.

Moses and God

A careful reading of the story of the Exodus, as it is recorded in the book by the same name as well as the Book of Numbers, reveals that Moses was a reluctant leader at times. On several occasions, he disagreed with what God had to say.

Moses didn't want the job in the first place. He was reluctant to give up watching his father-in-law's flock in order to take on such a daunting task. At the burning bush—the "job interview," so to speak—Moses gave God a list of excuses.

"Who am I?" (Exodus 3:11). *Are You sure I'm the man for the job? I'm just a simple, though well-educated, sheepherder. I'm not one who can go speak to powerful men.*

However, God said in effect, "You're the man. Stop worrying; I'll be with you every step of the way."

Moses responded, "What if they do not believe me or listen to me?" (4:1). *What if they don't pay attention to me? If they ignore me, I'll fail. That would be so humiliating!*

God assured Moses that He would multiply the common things he had into resources that would help the powerful ones understand. Two quick demonstrations—a staff turned into a snake and back into a staff and a hand made leprous and then healed immediately—proved to Moses that God had miracles in mind.

Still, Moses quibbled. "O LORD, I have never been eloquent. . . . I am slow of speech and tongue" (4:10). *I can't speak very well. I'm no public speaker.*

God: "Relax. I'll write your speeches."

Unconvinced, Moses tried yet another time. "O LORD, please send someone else to do it" (4:13). *Can't You look in that big stack of résumés on Your desk and find someone else more qualified? Oh, please, please, please?*

God's anger flashed. "No! I picked you. Now get going. But I will let your brother Aaron help you." End of conversation; time to get to work.

Yet, that was not the last time Moses had a conflict with the Lord. A couple times Moses complained about the people God had chosen him to lead. When they were grumbling about the lack of water, Moses asked God, "What am I to do with these people? They are almost ready to stone me" (Exodus 17:4). When the people grew tired of eating manna and quail, Moses got fed up with their wailing. He lashed out at God. "Why have you brought this trouble on your servant? What have I done to displease you that you put the burden of all these people on me? . . . I cannot carry all these people by myself; the burden is too heavy for me" (Numbers 11:11, 14). In effect, he said, "If this is the way You're going to treat me, I quit!"

On another occasion, Moses questioned God's methods. "You have been telling me, 'Lead these people,' but you have not let me know whom you will send with me" (Exodus 33:12). However, God, as any good leader should, reassured Moses that he was not in this endeavor alone. "My Presence will go with you, and I will give you rest" (33:14).

Our Problems with the Boss

Sometimes we may be reluctant followers of our earthly supervisors, as Moses was with God. Sometimes we will have problems getting along with those in authority over us. There may be several reasons why this happens.

We may feel inadequate. We might think that the boss's expectations for our job performance may overwhelm the resources we have. Then our conflict with the leader may come in the form of a litany of excuses. "I don't have the tools I need to do my job right." "I don't have the authority to accomplish that." "I can't talk in front of a group of strangers." "Anyone could do this better than I can."

We may feel that the boss's demands are unreasonable. It seems like our supervisors expect us to get 80 hours of work done in 40 hours. And they never want to pay for overtime! Or the boss acts like we don't have a family to go home to at night or a life outside the office. All he or she expects from us is work, work, work! And we can't count the number of times we have heard someone say in such a situation, "They don't pay me enough to do all this!"

We may think the leader doesn't know enough about the job. Sometimes it is true that the workers know more about a certain task than the supervisor. An example from one veteran's military experience makes this clear.

It is not difficult to visualize the conflict that can arise when a 33-year-old gunnery sergeant, with 15 years of service, has to work for a 25-year-old lieutenant, with one year of active duty. When I was in Vietnam in 1968, a new lieutenant reported into the command. He refused to accept anything that was said by enlisted men. The lieutenant attempted to prove he was better able to make decisions without any assistance from enlisted personnel. On the first day, the gunny said, "Lieutenant, we will be hit with enemy mortar and rocket fire tonight, and I can guarantee you will be wounded."

About 9:00 P.M. the nightly bombardment began. The last person into the bunker was the lieutenant. After the shelling stopped, the gunny went around to make sure everyone was safe and unhurt. The lieutenant had been hit in a couple places by shrapnel.

For the rest of his time in the unit, the lieutenant listened to what gunny had to say, and even sought him out for assistance in making some decisions.

Finally, *conflicts with those in authority over us may simply be an attitude problem.* For Christians, unhealthy attitudes should be examined under the light of the Holy Spirit. Ephesians 6 can help us in this. Though our employer-employee associations are not the slave-master connections of Paul's day, the words are still instructive for Christians.

> Slaves, obey your earthly masters with respect and fear, and with sincerity of heart, just as you would obey Christ. Obey them not only to win their favor when their eye is on you, but like slaves of Christ, doing the will of God from your heart. Serve wholeheartedly, as if you were serving the Lord, not men, because you know that the Lord will reward everyone for whatever good he does, whether he is slave or free (6:5-8).

Regardless of the situation between the boss and the worker, these three characteristics should be evident in a Christian:

- Obey orders with respect, fear, and sincerity.
- Obey your employer as if God were giving the orders.
- Give everything you have to the task.

We need to say one more thing before we move on. Conflict with a supervisor can be healthy. It can be the impetus for finding ways to better communicate and share ideas. It can even lead to finding more efficient ways to accomplish the goals everyone wants to see achieved. As we learned in the discussion in chapter 1, there are four levels of conflict—problem-solving, disagreement, contest, and relational warfare. Examine the situation and see if the conflict is at a level to bring good for all concerned out of it.

Moses and the Israelites

Moses had a problem that many supervisors have faced. The Israelites did not want to follow him at certain points in the journey. More than once, Moses had disgruntled persons on his hands.

Then Moses led Israel from the Red Sea and they went into the Desert of Shur. For three days they traveled in the desert without finding water. When they came to Marah, they could not drink its water because it was bitter. . . . So *the people grumbled against Moses,* saying, "What are we to drink?" (Exodus 15:22-24, emphasis added).

The whole Israelite community set out from the Desert of Sin, traveling from place to place as the LORD commanded. They camped at Rephidim, but there was no water for the people to drink. So *they quarreled with Moses* and said, "Give us water to drink" (Exodus 17:1-2, emphasis added).

When the constant diet of manna and quail became distasteful, the Israelite grievance committee was not bashful about questioning Moses' intentions. "If only we had died by the LORD'S hand in Egypt! There we sat around pots of meat and ate all the food we wanted, but you have brought us out into this desert to starve this entire assembly to death" (Exodus 16:3).

Later, when 10 out of 12 scouts claimed that the Israelites could not possibly defeat the people who already lived in Canaan, the people were ready to fire Moses, choose another leader, and return to the "security" of Egypt (see Numbers 13:31—14:4). On the sea, we call that "mutiny." At work, we call it "jumping off a sinking ship." However we phrase it, it amounts to conflict between the leaders and the followers.

Moses did not allow the people's negative words to derail the mission. Rather, he demonstrated humility. "Moses and Aaron fell facedown in front of the whole Israelite assembly gathered there" (Numbers 14:5). Then they all listened to a motivational speech by the two honest scouts, which reminded the people of the purpose of their journey (see v. 9).

It didn't solve the problems immediately, but it was a step in the right direction. As we know, the Israelites did occupy the Promised Land many years later, under Joshua's leadership, and with none of the original fathers still alive. There is a note of hope here we should not overlook in the midst of any conflict: God's purposes will never be ultimately thwarted.

Words with the Workers

When we have difficulties with those who work for us, there can be several causes.

Perhaps we have poorly communicated our mission. Troops cannot successfully follow the sound of a confused bugle call. We need to be clear when we discuss our goals and plans with those who will help us make them become reality.

Maybe our workers have different values and goals. Again, good communication will clear up such misunderstandings.

Possibly there are personality differences. Some such clashes can be overcome with lots of prayer and understanding. Occasionally the differences will be so great that the relationship becomes unworkable.

Sometimes employees simply refuse to comply with company rules and policies. If this is the cause of the conflict, it is very difficult to salvage the situation without a change of heart on the employee's part. Perhaps intentionally building relationships with employees and helping them understand that they are valuable parts of the team will prevent such rebellion.

As long as the discord has not reached an irreconcilable point because of stubborn rebellion, good can come from disagreement with those who work for us. It comes in the form of improved communication. We can listen to their feedback, even if it is couched in grumbling terms. We can hear their ideas and adopt as many as possible. And we can learn what we need to do to empower them to do their jobs well.

A couple of other ideas will go a long way to improve employer/employee relations. Management should live by the same rules and set an example of the work ethic as employees are asked to follow. And a good manager will let employees know that he or she cares about their personal situations and problems.

The apostle Paul, after telling slaves how to behave toward their masters, told masters: "Treat your slaves in the same way" (Ephesians 6:9). The "same way" involves respect, sincerity, wholehearted effort, and devotion to Christ.

Moses and His Relatives

We are never alone on the journey of life. There are other people inhabiting the same world where we live. Often we experience friction with those fellow travelers.

Moses was no exception. His brother Aaron and his sister Miriam accompanied him on the Exodus from Egypt. Each of them had at least one clash with Moses' leadership.

When Miriam and Aaron were unhappy with the Cushite woman Moses had married, they questioned his leadership. In effect, they said, "Aren't we just as good at leading as Moses? Does God only speak to him and not to us as well?" (see Numbers 12:1-2).

While Moses was gone up the mountain receiving the Ten Commandments, Aaron took matters in his own hands and nearly led the people to destruction. The golden calf made from melted jewelry was both an act of rebellion against Moses' leadership and an act of idolatry before God. This unlawful act nearly destroyed the people of Israel. To use modern terms, it nearly bankrupted the company and put them out of business.

In fact, God wanted Moses to step aside so He could destroy them and start over with only Moses to build a great nation. Moses pleaded with the Lord, with the result that "the LORD relented and did not bring on his people the disaster he had threatened" (Exodus 32:14).

Disagreements with Coworkers

There is more to conflict at work than just difficulties between supervisor and worker. Conflict that exerts the most pressure in our workday lives comes from and with the people we work with day in and day out. It is one thing to have an occasional run-in with the boss, which may be difficult but is generally over in a short period of time. It is a completely different situation when the dust-up is with the person you sit next to or work alongside for eight hours a day.

In many situations, "politics" is the main reason for discord among coworkers. In a highly competitive environment, each person has a desire to get ahead of everyone else. Attempting to do that, some persons will do and say almost anything, causing extreme distress for others.

However, even in less competitive situations, conflicts with coworkers are nearly unavoidable because of human foibles. Persons will act out in order to satisfy their needs, whether consciously or not. Every reason discussed in chapter 3 is informative here: People behave toward each other out of needs for power, to be right, for significance, for meaning, for connection, or for self-preservation. The resulting acts may be bizarre in the extreme or mildly irritating. Still, it is an environment every worker must overcome.

Is there a Christian response to such goings-on in workplaces? Yes, and the apostle Paul has passed it on to us. "Do not repay anyone evil for evil. Be careful to do what is right in the eyes of everybody. If it is possible, as far as it depends on you, live at peace with everyone" (Romans 12:17-18). These are not easy words to put into practice, but they are vital to our Christian witness in a disruptive marketplace.

There is a danger if we do not apply Paul's words to our relationships at work. Disagreements with coworkers, though seemingly minor, have the potential of escalating into deep resentments and bitterness. The only thing that can prevent such escalation is forgiveness, and forgiving is not easy to do.

Peter knew forgiveness is not easy, and he wanted to find out what the limits of his patience should be. So he asked Jesus how many times he should forgive, offering what he considered to be a generous number, "Up to seven times?" (Matthew 18:21).

Jesus surprised Peter with His answer. "Not seven times, but seventy-seven times" (v. 22). The text is not clear; Jesus might have meant seventy times seven, or 490 times! Whatever the actual number, the point is clear. There is no limit to the number of times a Christian must forgive, though we may feel that "enough is enough."

Furthermore, Colossians 3:13 applies to Christians in all situations, including work. "Bear with each other and forgive whatever grievances you may have against one another. Forgive as the Lord forgave you." Yes, that is a stricter rule than the world follows, but it is essential in order for the peace of Christ to reign in our everyday lives.

Conclusion

Since conflict in one form or another seems inevitable, perhaps forgiveness is the key to overcoming discord at work or anywhere in our life. One man's testimony bears this out.

How much has God forgiven me? Jesus predicated my ability to love others on how much I have been forgiven. I will never forget the day I admitted to God that He was right, and I had been wrong. The cleansing I felt involved my entire being. God's forgiveness was complete. True, I felt an enormous load drop off me, but I also felt the overpowering realization that I was loved and was important to someone. Someone cared for me enough to show me a better way of life; to forgive me for sins committed and life lived wrong.

Amazingly, things I had thought important no longer seemed important. At work, I realized how easy it is to major on minor things. What had seemed important just the day before no longer carried much weight. The little things my coworkers did that caused me irritation no longer mattered to me.

How damaging conflict will be at work, or in our daily lives, depends on how we react to the conflict. It is not easy to be a peacemaker, but it is well worth the effort.

Scriptures Cited: Exodus 3:11; 4:1, 10, 13; 15:22-24; 16:3; 17:1-2, 4; 32:14; 33:12, 14; Numbers 11:11, 14; 12:1-2; 13:31—14:5, 9; Matthew 18:21-22; Romans 12:17-18; Ephesians 6:5-9; Colossians 3:13

About the Author: Dr. Everett Leadingham is editor of the Dialog Series. Terry Pinkerton contributed to this chapter.

CHAPTER 5

CONFLICT IS UNCOMFORTABLE

by DAN CROY

JESSICA CAME OUT of the conference room as if she had heard the fire alarm. Her papers and files were clutched to her chest. Her facial expression and posture gave the appearance that she needed to get somewhere in a hurry but really didn't know where to go. Someone asked her if there was a problem.

"These early morning staff meetings have just turned into turf wars between departments. Juan and Anna were arguing over the budget this morning and . . . well, things like this upset me so much the rest of my day is ruined. I just can't stand conflict, I guess. Even when I'm not involved it gets to me. We're not a team anymore. Everyone is fighting all the time. I don't know if I can keep doing this. My blood pressure won't take it."

Juan walked out talking to someone about the budget. He kept poking his finger at a file folder as he walked by.

"I'm confused. Anna and I were looking at the same figures in the meeting, but somehow she's got the idea that we can do it with less money. Where does she think we can get this type of work done for less money? I must not be communicating well today. I thought it was clear enough for anyone to understand. Well, I'll call her later and discuss it some more. Maybe I was trying so hard to move toward a decision I missed the point she was trying to make. I want to save money too, but we need to move on this thing before

the end of the month. I'm going to talk to a few more people to make sure we haven't missed anything on this. I agree
with Anna. We want to do this right the first time. Let's find
out if she could meet with us later today."

Anna came out of the conference room with a smile on
her face. She was walking briskly down the hall talking to
another person as they compared schedules.

"Let's plan to get with Juan as soon as possible. He's put
a lot of work into this thing, and we need to move toward a
decision. I love challenging him in meetings. When the two
of us go at it, fantastic energy and creativity develop. Sometimes he thinks putting a budget report in front of us is all it
takes to get things done. Of course, his work is always thor-
ough. There wasn't anything in the budget that needed to be
changed, as far as I saw. Still, no one will ever know until
ideas are challenged and the group process forces some debate and focused thought. I love playing the devil's advocate
in these meetings. It energizes me for the rest of the day.
We've got a good staff —a great bunch of people. Oh, by the
way, Jessica didn't look so good this morning. Is she coming
down with something?"

All three of these people were in the same meeting. They
represent different levels of comfort with conflict. One is en-
ergized. One is neutral. One is devastated. Why do people
respond differently to the same experience? Why, at one
time or another, is conflict so uncomfortable for everyone?

The English word "conflict" comes from the Latin root
"to strike together." When opposing views surface, the striking together can be quite uncomfortable. This discomfort
can lead to both positive and negative results.

We realize the positive side of conflict when we are moti-
vated to do something constructive in order to resolve it.
Putting on a sweater when the temperature drops in the
evening is a good example. When our morning clothes no
longer keep our bodies at a comfortable level, the conflict
begins. Our comfort level is in danger when the desired and

actual temperatures oppose one another. This "striking to-gether" informs us of the dilemma and motivates us to do something about it. We put a sweater on and the conflict is resolved. In this case, the discomfort of conflict is beneficial. It moves us toward right and good behavior.

Unfortunately, the Church is not immune from conflict and its various consequences. This human condition exists within groups of Christian people as well. Would the meeting described above be any different if it took place in a local church? Could it? Should it?

Some have suggested that many of us lack the skills to effectively manage the conflict that inevitably occurs in human relationships. When we become aware of an inadequacy within ourselves—such as our lack of skills in managing conflict—we become aware of our frailty, our humanness, our vulnerability. This realization produces fear. When we fear something, we tend to avoid it. Therefore, when we see conflict, think it may happen, or hear about it taking place, we go to any length to avoid it. If we are successful at avoiding these settings and situations long enough, the avoidance seems to be reinforced. To explain this another way: If we are aware that we don't know how to swim and this vulnerability frightens us enough, we will make sure we are never around water. We decline the invitation to take the ferry. We don't go boating with our friends. This kind of behavior is reinforced in that each day we are not in danger of drowning (since we're never around water) we can simply say "I'm not a water person."

It is unlikely that we will seek to gain additional skills or improve the ones we have as long as our avoidance behavior keeps us away from situations where we might need or even desire to learn how to deal with the issue. No wonder there are so many people like Jessica who constantly say, "I don't like conflict."

Why is conflict so uncomfortable? Why does it seem most of us are like Jessica rather than Juan and Anna?

Conflict Threatens Our Safety

The first time we saw or participated in a childhood shoving match or fistfight, we learned that people in conflict can hurt others. We've learned through experience and observation that things can get out of hand quickly and somebody could go home with a bruised lip, a black eye, or worse. It is natural to want to avoid situations that threaten us physically. Just as we run to avoid an object falling in our direction, we run physically and emotionally from situations we perceive are threatening.

Past situations of physical or emotional abuse can produce triggers in our brains that simply warn us when similar settings exist. Many times the Jessicas of the world have some sort of abuse in their background. The experience of hearing someone raise his or her voice or pound a fist will set off the alarms in their memories that cue avoidance behaviors. Some people experience physical symptoms that make it necessary to leave the setting where conflict is taking place.

Even when we are not in a physically threatening situation, our bodies sometimes behave as if we are ready to run or fight. Our stomachs tighten, our heart rates increase, and our senses are heightened. We are uncomfortable because our bodies are telling our brains, "Watch out! Somebody could get hurt! Get out before it gets worse!"

Conflict Threatens Our Emotional Security

Closely related to the physical aspects of the human condition is our desire and need for emotional security within our relationships. We develop trust for the other person. We can feel free to take the risks involved in being vulnerable. We want and need to know that our work team, our family, our church fellowship, the committee, our neighbors are all OK being together. We want everyone to just get along. We want assurances that we are doing what leads to peaceful coexistence.

When our dog bites the neighbor's child, when coworkers begin to fight over an issue, when one parent and child begin to have a battle of the wills, it seems as if our emotional security is threatened. We feel our "OKness" is threatened.

It is uncomfortable when, within the context of a close relationship, we experience betrayal, hurt, and anger directed toward us from the very persons we trusted the most. This results in feelings of anger. If this anger is not handled properly, it can lead to destructive, dysfunctional, or sinful behavior. It seems that interpersonal conflict is the most painful because of the personal nature of the interaction between people who are, at times, confused as to whether a problem or a person is being attacked.

The conflict between husband and wife or parent and child can threaten our emotional security to the point that we will do anything to put an end to the conflict. Sometimes it seems safer to put up with the dysfunctional, settle for the abusive, and get comfortable with the incompetent— all in the name of avoiding conflict. Too many people live their daily lives in terrible situations because they have convinced themselves that "this is as good as it gets." If we ask if they are happy or satisfied with the way things are, they will answer in the negative. They know their lives are miserable. Yet, they continue to fight change because they can't bear the thought of more conflict. "Going with the flow" seems the way to go.

Conflict Threatens Our Comfort Zones

The two needs for adequacy ("Am I OK?") and security ("Are we OK?") exist in all of us. Whenever these are threatened, we react. The human systems we have established in relationships, social structures, and organizations may not be effective, efficient, or healthy, but they are what we know. We are used to doing things the way we've always done them. We're comfortable with it. After all, it worked so well for so long, why change now?

When something or someone announces that our systems will be changing, we perceive that as a threat, and we resist the change. Conflict in the Church has often followed this path. We allow our place of service to become our identity. We're OK as long as we are doing our job. However, if someone comes along who can do it better or the job is eliminated altogether, we're no longer OK.

We also create processes, systems, and even buildings to become our security. The program or building becomes more important than its desired objective. The *methods* become confused as *mission*. When someone suggests the old sanctuary become a youth center, some people hear it as if the leadership were denying a basic doctrinal truth.

There is usually no conflict associated with the mission of the Church. Who's going to speak against obeying the Great Commission (see Matthew 28:18-20)? The *what* of the church rarely creates conflict. Win the lost and minister to the saints (see John 13:34-35). However, when we talk about the *how* of accomplishing this mission, the conflicts begin. From the color of the carpet to music styles during worship, comfort zones are breeched and some people leave the local church simply to avoid the conflict.

Three Forces Behind Our Comfort Levels

The model following is a graphic depiction of at least three forces that determine our comfort level with conflict. Our principles, personality, and perspective all play an important role in the midst of conflict because they drive our thoughts, attitudes, and behaviors.

Principles

Principles include such things as our worldview and faith as Christians, our ethical standards, moral beliefs, and the overall principles by which we determine what is right or wrong, true or false. These principles influence our comfort level with conflict by driving our motivation whether to get

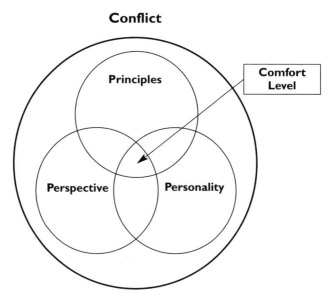

© 2003 Daniel A. Croy, Ed.D.

involved in or even initiate the conflict. When an issue arises between people regarding appropriate behavior in society—political or religious issues—it is fairly easy to observe those involved whose principles are being challenged.

Personality

Personality here can represent our temperament, personality, or *persona*. This includes our ability to invest emotional energy into relationships and the communication that's needed to sustain them. Our ability to articulate our thoughts and emotions is included here as well. Sometimes conflict between two people seems to be resolved or, at least, to come to a halt, not because the issue was settled but more likely the more articulate, dramatic, persuasive personality out-talked the other person. Certain cultures present a "personality" of sorts when faced with conflict. For instance, some cultures care less about the specific topic and place more value on who loses face in the interaction. The one who loses his or her "cool" first actually loses the conflict.

Perspective

Our perspective includes our views on the issue, how we perceive the other people involved in the conflict, our knowledge and beliefs about the issue, and how important the outcome is to us if and when the conflict is resolved. Our beliefs about conflict itself are important here as well.

The Faith Factor

The principle, personality, and perspective components above can also represent our *will, emotions,* and *intellect.* These are aspects of our human condition that are not designed to be the final authorities in our lives. The follower of the Lord Jesus Christ surrenders his or her will to God's will. Our emotions are too fickle to be trusted, and our intellect is limited and fraught with errors.

When we review how conflict threatens our safety, security, and comfort levels, we realize again that the fallen world in which we live temporarily is not to be trusted to provide what we truly need.

- When our wills are surrendered to God's will, conflict is seen as a tool to shape us, teach us, and mature us into the image of Christ (see Hebrews 12:7-11).
- When we trust our emotions and intellect less and choose to follow the Holy Spirit's leading, our responses to conflict will be more Christlike (see Proverbs 3:5-8; Philippians 2:1-11).
- When we acknowledge and accept that our safety, security, and comfort can ultimately come from God alone, we can accept conflict realistically and approach it with faith that surpasses the understanding of mere mortal men and women (see 2 Timothy 1:7; 1 Peter 5:7; Psalm 119:52, 76; Proverbs 1:33).

When conflict occurs, as it will in this life, our comfort

level with it is influenced by many factors. Regardless of our initial response to it, the most important factor is our faith. No matter what the issue, no matter how high the stakes, our approach should be based on our faith in a sovereign God who loves us, knows what's best for us, and has a plan for our lives. He is to be trusted with the conflict in our lives. He is the One who can equip us to deal with it effectively—even when we're not comfortable.

We are called to be committed to the Lord—not necessarily to be comfortable with conflict.

Scriptures Cited: Psalm 119:52, 76: Proverbs 1:33; 3:5-8; Matthew 28:18-20; John 13:34-35; Philippians 2:1-11; 2 Timothy 1:7; Hebrews 12:7-11; 1 Peter 5:7

About the Author: Dr. Dan Croy teaches at Point Loma Nazarene University in San Diego, California.

CHAPTER 6

GOVERNING AUTHORITIES

by CHIP RICKS

I GREW UP IN a small town of about 3,500 people in Texas. We had one telephone in our house and one black-and-white television. We never locked the doors, and only screens protected the windows of our home. Since there was no air-conditioning, most windows were open at night. We felt safe. Our neighbors knew that even when we were not at home, they were welcome to come in to borrow a cup of sugar or anything else they needed.

We had only one law officer in our town. He patrolled the streets and made sure that all teenagers headed for home before the 10 o'clock curfew. He usually caught up with us at the corner drug store and enjoyed a soda or ice cream with us. I do not remember any teenager ever being arrested in our town, although parents were sometimes called when one of us failed to follow what that community considered to be proper behavior.

On Sundays, the churches were open, and all stores were closed. Although the theater once tried opening on Sunday afternoons, few people went, and it soon closed. The home-room classes in our public school began each morning with prayer, and a scripture verse for the week was written on the chalkboard. The Pledge of Allegiance was recited, followed by the singing of a patriotic song. The Ten Commandments were in a large frame hanging on the wall, just inside the door of the school for all to see. Courses in the history of our nation and the laws of our government were required for high school graduation.

Life has changed in my hometown. It's a different world now.

Today all over the nation doors and windows are locked, and our homes are protected by alarm systems with lines to the local police. Law enforcement officers have multiplied to patrol our streets and highways. Teen violence has exploded; some even arrested for murder. Burglaries, rapes, and murders occur every minute. The government must spend billions of dollars each year to protect us.

Where Are We Headed?

As we look at society over the last few decades, it is easy to spot changes that are alarming to many Christians.

Prayer and the Bible: Prayer in public schools was a common activity until 1962, when the United States Supreme Court declared it unconstitutional. According to the 1965 decision in *Reed vs. Van Hoven,* a student may pray over his or her lunch—but only silently. Since 1986, opening and closing prayers at graduation ceremonies have been prohibited.

In 1963, because of the case of *Murray vs. Curlett,* the Bible was taken out of public schools. In 1980, *Stone vs. Graham* caused the Ten Commandments to be taken down from public school walls. It causes some to wonder if these actions have had some bearing on the teenage crimes now being committed in schools.

Abortion: Experts say that partial-birth abortions have increased 300 percent in the last few years. In January 2003, a pro-life activist group delivered 200,000 petitions to Congress, asking that *Roe vs. Wade,* which allows such abortions, be repealed. These petitions arrived during a major pro-choice summit held in Washington, D.C., celebrating the 30th anniversary of the *Roe vs. Wade* decision.

Religious Symbols: In Lompoc, California, one congregation located in the center of town voted to ring their church bells every day at noon. While some residents have expressed concern that this action is inappropriate, believers see it as a great blessing. What a joy it is to hear those church bells ring out.

In the same town, a large cross sits high on a hill overlooking the main street of the town. While some people have asked that it be removed, the cross still stands for all to see. Nevertheless, the question is still open—for how long?

In Groom, Texas, the second largest cross in the world stands alone on the flat grassy plain. It is the gift of one man, who spent his life savings of $300,000 to build it. Some of the people in Groom are thankful for this strong reminder of the power of the Cross. Others, of course, are offended by it all.

Crosses have frequently caused conflict, but not always as a symbol of Christianity. The burning of crosses in the South has for many years been a means of causing fear and terrorizing citizens. Recently, a black citizen moved his family out of Virginia Beach, Virginia after two white neighbors tried to burn a four-foot cross in his yard.

Historically, the Supreme Court has protected the rights of citizens to burn crosses, the flag, and other symbols of controversy. Now, the Supreme Court is considering how far states may go to discourage the burning of crosses, a practice rooted in racial hatred but given free speech protection.

Religious symbols all across the United States are being removed by court order. Since 1969, it has been unconstitutional for a cross to be erected as a war memorial. Fewer Christian symbols are seen today in Christmas celebrations. Manger scenes have virtually vanished from military bases and public places. Generic "Happy Holidays" signs have replaced more traditional wording.

All these changes are the result of conflicting viewpoints. Christians must look for guidance to know when to obey and when to disobey, when to act and when to remain silent.

A Long Way from Where We Started

In the founding days of the United States, it seems that religious beliefs had a more accepted influence on governmental leaders than they do today.

In 1787, as 55 men gathered to write the Constitution of the United States, Benjamin Franklin stood and proposed a resolution to some of the minor disagreements that were beginning to occur. He suggested that "prayers imploring the assistance of Heaven and its blessing on our deliberation be held in this assembly every morning before we proceed to business."[1] His proposition was accepted, and the group created the historic document.

On April 30, 1789, standing on the outdoor balcony of Federal Hall in New York City, George Washington placed his right hand on the Bible and took the oath of office as the first president of the United States. Church bells rang. Artillery was fired. And the crowd shouted with joy and high expectations for the first administration under the new Constitution.

In his inaugural address to Congress, Washington stated, "No people can be bound to acknowledge and adore the invisible hand which conducts the affairs of men more than the people of the United States." Then he warned that we cannot expect God to continue to bless our nation if we as a people disregard "the eternal rules of order and right, which Heaven itself has ordained."[2] Following his address, the president, along with his staff and members of Congress, moved to St. Paul's Chapel where the congressional chaplain led them in a worship service.

However, the 20th century brought many changes in government. Religious principles are not readily identifiable as the basis on which government is run. Hardly anyone would consider us a Christian nation. More and more, we are seeing conflict between Christian citizens and government authorities.

A Christian Attitude Toward Government

Though we are writing this chapter from our experience in the United States, Christians the world over must deal with governing authorities. Just as the Roman government Paul was writing about was not a democracy, so not every Christian has the freedom enjoyed in North America. Still, there are some biblical Christian attitudes that can be universally applied.

When Paul wrote his letters, Rome ruled the western world. Nero, the cruel emperor who murdered his brother, his mother, and two of his wives, was considered a god. Many Christians died because they refused to say that the emperor was divine. Conflict between Christians and the Roman government in the first few centuries after Jesus was primarily over worship of the emperor and worship of Christ.

Political revolution was not the purpose of the first Christians' conflict with government. While it must have been hard for the early Christians, several New Testament writers said God wanted believers to have deep respect for government. Peter wrote, "Submit yourselves for the Lord's sake to every authority instituted among men: whether to the king . . . or to governors. . . . Live as free men, but do not use your freedom as a cover-up for evil; live as servants of God. Show proper respect to everyone: Love the brotherhood of believers, fear God, honor the king" (1 Peter 2:13-14, 16-17). Paul told Titus, "Remind the people to be subject to rulers and authorities, to be obedient, to be ready to do whatever is good, to slander no one, to be peaceable and considerate, and to show true humility toward all" (Titus 3:1-2).

In Romans 13, Paul helps us understand what a Christian attitude toward government authority should be. "Everyone must submit . . . to the governing authorities. . . . The authorities that exist have been *established by God.* Consequently, . . . rebels . . . will bring judgment on themselves" (vv. 1-2, emphasis added).

Paul explains in the next two verses that if we do good, we have no reason to fear government. Only when we do evil should we be afraid, because then the government becomes "God's servant, an agent of wrath to bring punishment on the wrongdoer" (v. 4). Paul concludes, "Therefore, it is necessary to submit to the authorities, not only because of possible punishment but also because of conscience" (v. 5).

This is a difficult idea for those in democratic societies to understand. We feel that government leaders have authority because the *people* granted it to them through election. Yet, the biblical view is that God established government for the good of all people. The fact that monarchs and dictators have abused their power does not negate the divine will of good for all persons.

Clearly, we are called to obey the laws of our government. We live in a community, and government provides many things we could not provide for ourselves. However, as Christians, we are citizens of two domains: the realm of God and the realm of the world. This often creates a conflict. Jesus clarified our allegiance to both when He said, "Give to Caesar what is Caesar's, and to God what is God's" (Matthew 22:21). Jesus made this statement in answer to the question, "Is it right to pay taxes to Caesar or not?" (v. 17). Certainly, we must not refuse to pay our taxes. Neither can we refuse to obey traffic laws, license our vehicles, or follow building codes and laws governing our businesses. We are commanded to respect our government.

Still, we often live in tension between obedience to the government and obedience to God. When government leaders enact laws or make decisions which conflict with what we know to be right by God's principles, "we must obey God rather than men" (Acts 5:29). We have many examples in God's Word of brave persons who chose to "obey God rather than men." Esther risked death by breaking the royal court's protocol to speak boldly to the king and thereby save the Jews from Haman's plot to destroy them (see Esther

4:7—5:2). Daniel's three well-known friends—Shadrach, Meshach and Abednego—refused to obey Nebuchadnezzar and bow to his idol, an order in conflict with the first and second commandments (see Daniel 3:14-18). Peter and John continued to preach Christ crucified in spite of the Sanhedrin's order to cease (see Acts 5:28-29).

There have been modern-day conflicts as well. As Christians, could we have kept silent when the Nazis ordered the death of Jews in Germany? Or would we have disobeyed the government, as many German citizens did, and helped some Jewish people escape capture? We face similar challenges today; we need only look around us. When our consciences are stirred because human law contradicts God's law, rather than for selfish human reasons, then we can go against the government and work for God's justice.

What Can We Do?

Sometimes Christians are faced with conflict because what the government requires is at odds with God's law. At other times, Christians are caught in the friction between differing political viewpoints in an increasingly pluralistic society. As citizens, what can we do to support the government which God has given us?

The Legal System: Whenever possible, we must rely on the courts of the land to enforce the law and settle disputes. Often, the courts are a peaceful means of restoring justice to those who have been unfairly treated. Recently, for example, a California auto insurer was fined $200,000 for unfair claims settlement practices. In another case, Florida policyholders were awarded $9 million in compensation from two insurance companies who were charged with unfair practices—using race to set premium prices.

Prayer: Of course, we must pray. Paul wrote, "I urge, then, first of all, that requests, prayers, intercession and thanksgiving be made for everyone—for kings and all those in authority, that we may live peaceful and quiet lives in all godliness and holiness" (1 Timothy 2:1-2). We should pray for leaders at every level of government—local, state, and federal. Daily we should ask God to give wisdom to those government officials who make the decisions which concern each of us. And we should give thanks that God still rules over nations and is the supreme authority.

What if we live where the government is corrupt and oppresses its people, especially Christians? Should we pray for evil rulers? If we live by what Jesus taught in the Sermon on the Mount, the answer is yes. "Love your enemies and pray for those who persecute you" (Matthew 5:44). And the same advice applies to us for those who disagree, however heatedly, with our political views in a democracy.

Citizenship: If we are fortunate enough to live in a democracy, we should exercise the rights of citizenship. Vote. Volunteer time to work for the election of godly men and women. Keep informed and think through the issues being voted on in government. Sign petitions requesting justice wherever we see it being violated from a Christian perspective. Encourage our representatives through phone calls, letters, and E-mails to vote for issues that square with principles God makes clear in His Word. If we feel it is necessary, join with others in a peaceful demonstration for an issue we know to be right. Even seeking political office is an option, if God leads in that direction.

Jesus characterized Christians as "the salt of the earth" and "the light of the world" (Matthew 5:13-14). He urged, "Let your light shine before men, that they may see your good deeds and praise your Father in heaven" (v. 16). In many ways as Christians in an increasingly secular culture, we are "aliens and strangers in the world" (1 Peter 2:11). Yet, each of us is a citizen of some earthly nation. As such, it is our responsibility to work to bring about change in government structures that are in conflict with God's laws.

Christians should be the best and most active citizens in the affairs of their nation, working to resolve conflict. Or as a prophet once asked and answered, "What does the LORD require of you? To act justly and to love mercy and to walk humbly with your God" (Micah 6:8). Nothing more needs to be done.

Notes:

1. Peter Marshall and David Manuel, *The Light and the Glory* (Grand Rapids: Fleming H. Revell, 1977), 343.

2. David Barton, *Original Intent* (Aledo, Tex.: WallBuilder Press, 2002), 114.

Scriptures Cited: Esther 4:7—5:2; Daniel 3:14-18; Micah 6:8; Matthew 5:13-14, 16, 44; 22:17, 21; Acts 5:28-29; Romans 13:1-5; 1 Timothy 2:1-2; Titus 3:1-2; 1 Peter 2:11, 13-14, 16-17

About the Author: Chip Ricks, a college English teacher for 24 years, is now a freelance writer, retreat speaker, and teacher of adults at her church.

CHAPTER 7

IS CONFLICT NECESSARY?

by STEPHEN J. LENNOX

THE ATMOSPHERE in the boardroom grew still and tense. One of the board members, a military veteran, had just voiced his concern that there was no American flag in the sanctuary. "We had flags from all those other countries for the mission service, but the American flag was missing!"

To my right, I could see my friend stiffen and lean forward. "I don't think we need to display the flag in church," he answered. "We are Christians first, then citizens. Nazi Germany got that wrong and look what happened to them."

The argument that followed was as heated as I've ever seen on the board. Are such conflicts really necessary?

"Conflict Is Not Necessary"

There are many godly, wonderful Christians who feel that conflict has no place in the life of the believer. We should turn the other cheek and give to all who ask. We should be as mild as Jesus, who did not resist as wicked people struck Him, spat on Him, and even crucified Him. The importance of maintaining our Christlike spirit outweighs our personal rights to self-defense.

If we should live without conflict with the unbeliever, they would ask, how much more should tranquility prevail in our relationships with fellow believers? "The fruit of the Spirit is love, joy, peace, patience, kindness, goodness, faithfulness, gentleness and self-control" (Galatians 5:22-23). What possible cause for conflict could arise between two believers who have the Spirit of God living in them?

Those who take this approach make several assumptions. They assume that all conflict is dangerous, damaging, and always the result of sin. They also associate conflict with anger, as if the two are inseparable. The Holy Spirit, they assume, wants to eliminate all conflict from the life of the believer.

These assumptions are partly right. The Spirit did come to bring peace to the life of the believer, but also conflict. Jesus taught on one occasion, "Do not suppose that I have come to bring peace to the earth. I did not come to bring peace, but a sword" (Matthew 10:34).

While some conflict can be dangerous, even deadly, it is sometimes the only path to healing and wholeness. Those in conflict are often angry, but not always, nor is anger always wrong. Still, to the extent that conflict results from sinful behavior, conflict and the sin that caused it should be avoided at all costs.

Conflict Is Inevitable

Realistically, however, conflict is an inevitable part of everyday life, even church life. It doesn't always mean sin is present; it just means people are present. People who, without sinning, express their disagreement. Look around: Conflict is everywhere. Weather results from the interaction (conflict) of low-pressure systems with high-pressure systems and cold fronts with warm fronts. Look inside: White blood cells conflict with germs. Blood is forced against the walls of vessels to accomplish its purpose. Digestive juices break down food. Every step we take is a complex process of conflicting actions of muscles, bones, and tendons. Our bodies operate by controlled conflict.

Look at the past: All great moments in history, including biblical history, have been accompanied by conflict. The call of Abraham meant a break from his family and polytheistic past. The Israelites came out of Egypt only after costly conflict. David became king only after the end of Saul's dynasty. The Incarnation brought light into the darkness, and the

Cross and Resurrection broke the back of death and hell. Essential doctrines of the faith were settled in great Church councils amid dispute and argument. Only through conflict did we experience the Protestant Reformation and Wesley's revival in England. There had to be a Revolutionary War before there could be the United States, a Civil War before this could be a slavery-free country, and the Second World War to end Nazi aggression.

Conflict Is Even Beneficial

Conflict will be and ought to be an important part of the life of every believer. We need not look for it; conflict will come to us. It must, for conflict was designed by God to be an important part of His plan for us and for this world. It is one important way He intends to make us perfect, to help us mature into the persons He intends us to be. It is how He plans to accomplish His goal for humanity.

The New Testament writers predicted that there would be conflict. Through Peter, we learned there would be struggles with unbelievers, for "scoffers will come, scoffing and following their own evil desires. They will say, 'Where is this "coming" he promised? Ever since our fathers died, everything goes on as it has since the beginning of creation'" (2 Peter 3:3-4). Paul parted the curtain that separates flesh from spirit and identified such interpersonal conflicts as a struggle, "not against flesh and blood, but against the rulers, against the authorities, against the powers of this dark world and against the spiritual forces of evil in the heavenly realms" (Ephesians 6:12). Even Jesus, the Prince of Peace asked, "Do you think I came to bring peace on earth? No, I tell you, but division. From now on there will be five in one family divided against each other, three against two and two against three. They will be divided, father against son and son against father, mother against daughter and daughter against mother, mother-in-law against daughter-in-law and daughter-in-law against mother-in-law" (Luke 12:51-53).

Given the difference between spiritual light and spiritual darkness, conflict between them is inevitable. However, not all conflict should be seen as the result of spiritual warfare. Some conflict is designed by God to accomplish His purposes in us. Although he does not identify the benefits of conflict as coming from God, Jeffrey A. Kottler is convinced that not only are interpersonal conflicts to be expected, they are to be desired.

> In many ways, they are even necessary if we are ever to advance our knowledge and live with each other's differences. There is no sense in blaming ourselves, or anyone else, for getting us into arguments or disagreements; that is the logical consequence of taking a stand on issues that are important to us, of not compromising our standards in the face of pressure.[1]

God *wants* His people to experience conflict with others. Although often painful, conflict is often how God brings about the changes He desires. Kottler compares conflict to a journey. We want to get to our destination, for there we'll find what we've been seeking, perhaps a friendly welcome or a rewarding experience. Yet before we arrive, we must deal with many miles, cramped quarters, airline meals, sleepless hours, congested highways, and disgruntled fellow travelers. Until they invent a machine that "beams" us from one spot to another, we're stuck with such inconvenience. Conflict is like that journey. We may not love traveling—few do—but it is the only way to get from here to there. And "there" is where God wants us to be, both for our good and His glory.

Why Do People Disagree?

In earlier chapters, we've discovered some of the reasons conflict occurs. It is also safe to say that conflicts usually occur over four issues:

- Sometimes we fight over *facts*. We disagree about what is the most accurate information, like the right interpretation of Scripture.

- We fight over *methods,* how something should be done. When people quarrel about styles of worship, it is mostly about method.
- Sometimes the conflict is over *values.* The United States two-party political system is largely value-based. Should we have a lean and limited government or should we have a lot of government-funded social programs? This kind of question, though it has implications for facts and methods, is more about what we believe in and cherish.
- We also have conflicts about *goals.* When churches wrestle with whether to build a new building or go to multiple services in order to invest in ministry, these are conflicts that reveal our mission, our goals.

God designed and desires conflict so that in each of these areas—our facts, methods, values, and goals—we will conform more closely to His ideal. It may be easiest to understand God's plan if we look first at how conflict can improve us; second, at how it can improve those with whom we are in conflict; and third, how it can change the circumstances we share.

How Conflict Can Make Us Better

Safety Valve: One of the wonderful benefits of conflict is that it acts as a "release valve" to relieve tension and keep it from exploding into something dangerous and damaging. Ask any plumber to learn about the value of a release valve on a boiler. Without it, the pressure inside would become so great the boiler would burst and spray scalding water everywhere. The purpose of the valve is to release the pressure in small, harmless amounts and prevent the big explosion. By dealing with disagreements over facts, methods, values, and goals as they arise, pressure doesn't have a chance to build, and normal frustrations and tensions are expressed and resolved safely. Big blow-ups—the kind that give conflict a bad name—are the result of disagreements left unattended.

Better Self-understanding: On several occasions, the Book of Proverbs speaks of the value of rebuke:

- "A rebuke impresses a man of discernment more than a hundred lashes a fool" (17:10).
- "Rebuke a discerning man, and he will gain knowledge" (19:25*b*).
- "Wounds from a friend can be trusted, but an enemy multiplies kisses" (27:6).

When someone looks me in the eye and tells me I'm wrong, we're in conflict, but conflict which provides me with a mirror. Looking into that mirror helps me better understand myself. I can learn how I'm being perceived. Let's say I'm rebuked for being too critical. I never meant to be harsh; I thought I was only being funny. Yet because my friend was willing to confront me, I can be more self-aware, choosing my words and tone of voice more carefully. Even if I determine he is wrong in his rebuke, the process of self-evaluation can still be very helpful.

How we react to a rebuke can be very enlightening, as it reveals aspects of character. Those who are unwilling to listen to any word of correction should be especially concerned. Those who immediately accept rebuke without asking if it is true should check out their need to please everyone. When rebuked, we should ask what stung most deeply about the criticism. When confronted with a critical spirit, were we more concerned about not being liked or about hurting someone else by our words? Is it more important to find a way to defend ourselves or to learn how we could improve?

Conflict can also be enlightening when I'm the one who issues the rebuke. I initiated the conflict because I felt that I was right and the issue was worth the trouble. Even while it provides a moment to teach another, conflict is also a good time for me to learn. I can learn about myself by asking why I feel it necessary to confront my friend. In other words, when I find something worth a conflict, I have discovered one of my values. I can also learn something about myself by asking why I felt it necessary to confront this particular person, rather than someone else who was doing the same thing. Are my motives pure and other-centered, or do I confront from a need to show who's boss? Conflict can be a wonderfully enlightening, if sometimes painful moment.

Better Understanding of Issues: One of the great things about conflict is that it provides an opportunity to learn more. Every criticism has some grain of truth; learning to discover the truth is the mark of a wise person. Since conflicts are often over facts, they provide an opportunity to tell the rest of the story, the part we did not know or did not want to know.

Conflict also provides a way to peel back the facts and get at the underlying values and goals at stake. In early 2003, the United States was in conflict over whether or not to invade Iraq. The several conversations (that is, conflicts) I had with colleagues on this issue, helped me discover the moral issues which lay beneath it. Would this be a just war? Would it create a dangerous precedent in American foreign policy? What would be the consequences of inaction? Had we not had those conversations, I don't think I would have considered the deeper, value-level issues.

Change for the Better: In addition to greater insight into ourselves and into the issues, conflict also helps us actually become better persons. This makes it an indispensable tool in God's plan for our perfection. Learning more facts helps us make better decisions. Learning better methods helps us do our jobs more effectively. Hearing and incorporating correction helps us become better persons, with better values and goals.

Listening to how we confront, watching what works and what doesn't, helps us develop better skills of communication and persuasion. It helps develop problem-solving skills to avoid unnecessary conflict and conflict management skills when the inevitable arrives. If it is necessary, it should at least be beneficial.

Being more attentive through conflict to the dynamics of interpersonal interaction, I can improve my relationships. Kottler points out the benefits of conflict in moving one from a codependent relationship to one characterized by independence. "Conflict acts as a distancer between people who are overly close and need to create space between themselves—for both their sakes."[2] Conflict can also bring me closer to my friend as, through the conflict, I gain a better understanding of what really matters to him or her.

Conflict Helps Others Change

Up to this point, we have only been talking about how conflict can benefit us, but it can also be wonderfully helpful to others. I waited to talk about this, however, because what I'm going to say is so dangerous. I don't want a reader to think that since conflict is necessary and beneficial, he or she should become a crusader, beating up on others as an "angel of mercy." Conflict *can* benefit others, but *only* those who've first turned it to their own good are ready to employ it for others.

Conflict can reveal another's values. This is powerfully illustrated in the case of Judas as we meet him in John 12:1-8. Jesus was dining at the home of Lazarus when Mary, Lazarus's sister, began to anoint Jesus' feet with an expensive perfume. Judas, treasurer of the disciples, immediately protested. "Why wasn't this perfume sold and the money given to the poor?" (v. 5). John explains that Judas's concern was not for the poor, but for himself. The anointing created a conflict between Mary's values and those of Judas, revealing the latter for what he was. Sadly, Judas's values did not change and led him to his sorry end.

Jesus predicted that Christians would be persecuted—perhaps the most painful type of conflict—but that the persecution would be a witness to unbelieving rulers (see Luke 21:13). How can persecution lead to witness? By demonstrating the superior values of the Christians. Paul confronted Peter in Antioch, according to Galatians 2:11-21, because Peter's values and actions were wrong. Paul's courage to confront Peter, at that time the appointed and acknowledged leader of the church, left Peter and the whole church in a healthier state.

When Nathan confronted David for his sins with Bathsheba and Uriah (2 Samuel 12:1-13), it not only revealed David's self-centered values and murderous ways, it sent David to his knees in repentance. Conflict can prompt others to change for the better, whether better actions, better methods, better values, or better goals.

Conflict Makes Things Better

Few things get better without conflict. People do not break off unhealthy relationships, give up bad habits, or develop good ones without conflict. Ideas do not change without conflict. Ask Galileo or Copernicus or Luther or Wesley. Today's worship wars, although difficult, are helping the Church to rethink the true nature of worship and the Church.

People need conflict to grow, and so do churches. When I was a young pastor, I was forced into a confrontation with a leading layperson in the church. I was terrified of conflict and especially with someone so powerful, but I felt emboldened to stand firm. I'm so glad I did. The conflict led to his leaving the church, not by my choice but his. However, his departure breathed new life into the church, like opening a window in a hot, stuffy room. The church began to grow from that point on.

Conclusion

Conflict that arises from sin has no place in the Church, nor does conflict that proceeds from wrong motives or by wrong means. Yet, conflict is not the problem here; sin is. Conflict is inevitable. What is more important, conflict is necessary if God is going to do His work in our lives and in

His church. Our task is to find ways to use the conflict to better understand ourselves and the issues we face. We must allow conflict to change us and our world for the better.

Notes:

1. Jeffrey A. Kottler, *Beyond Blame* (San Francisco: Jossey-Bass, 1994), 162.
2. Kottler, 156.

Scriptures Cited: 2 Samuel 12:1-13; Proverbs 17:10; 19:25*b*; 27:6; Matthew 10:34; Luke 12:51-53; 21:13; John 12:1-8; Galatians 2:11-21; 5:22-23; Ephesians 6:12; 2 Peter 3:3-4

About the Author: Dr. Stephen Lennox is chair of the religion and philosophy department at Indiana Wesleyan University, Marion, Indiana.

CHAPTER **8**

MISUNDERSTANDINGS IN MARRIAGE

by LES & LESLIE PARROTT

"YOU'RE TRYING to change me," Leslie blurted out over a halfheartedly prepared dinner of macaroni and cheese.

"What are you talking about?" I demanded with as much pretense of piety and surprise as I could muster.

Truth is, I knew what she was talking about. And I was trying to change her. She knew it. I knew it. I just didn't want her to know that I knew it. It had been tense in our little apartment that day ever since both of us got home from work. What was the issue? I can barely remember now, 20 years later, but I know it had something to do with her not being as organized in the kitchen as I wanted her to be. I made some inane critical comment about not being able to find something I could always find in my kitchen growing up. Well, OK, it wasn't the first critical comment I'd made that week, or even that evening.

"I'm talking about the way you make snippy comments," Leslie said, as she tried to restrain her tears. "No matter what I do, it's not good enough."

"That's not true," I said defensively. "Give me one good example of how I'm so critical." That was a mistake. For the next several minutes, she put out specific examples, and then I responded exactly how reasonable my critical comment was. It was a game of mental Ping-Pong that no one would win. Actually, it was a fight. Our first fight as a married couple.

81

Finally, Leslie, her eyes rimmed with tears, said something to end the tiresome match. "The point is, I'm trying to be a good wife, and I feel like I'm disappointing you."

"You're not disappointing me," I quickly responded in an attempt to keep her from crying. It was too late. She buried her eyes in one of the linen napkins we'd received as a wedding gift. "You don't need to cry," I said, the way only a new husband would attempt to comfort his bride. The dinner was over, but Leslie's crying wasn't. I sat helplessly, not knowing what to do or where to go.

✻ ✻ ✻

I (Leslie), on the other hand, knew exactly where I wanted to go—back home. And I probably would have if Chicago hadn't been 2,000 miles away. The loneliness of that moment was palpable. Sitting in that tiny kitchen of that tiny apartment in the middle of the sprawling city of Los Angeles, beginning graduate school as well as a marriage, I wanted nothing more than to be somewhere safe and sound.

Sure, it's a kind of cliché, the new bride running home to Mom, but it wouldn't exist if it didn't contain a kernel of truth. Turns out a lot of new brides, as well as their new husbands, experience this urge in the aftermath of their first fight. We've seen it countless times with the countless newlywed couples we've counseled.

We know of a bride who, after having a big blowout, called her mom across town to come over and pick her up. "We're having a terrible fight, and I just want to come home." In 10 minutes, Dad was there to whisk the young woman back to the house. He took a meandering route back. When he finally pulled into the driveway, his daughter ran to the front door. Once inside, she found her husband standing alone in the living room. "What are you doing here?" she asked.

"Your mom came by as soon as you left and said she wanted me to come over." The young couple looked at each other with bewildered faces. Then they looked out the front window to see her mother and father driving away. That's when they both cracked up and soon forgot why they were fighting.

The message this seasoned couple was sending their daughter and son-in-law was clear: You can't run away to work out your problems. So, why do so many new couples want to do just that? Primarily because it feels so safe. When you are a new spouse who has hit the first jolt, you realize that not everything is going to go as planned. You feel uncertain. *Did I make a huge mistake?* Suddenly, the ground becomes shaky, and you wonder if there's a place for you in this new relationship. One thing you know, there's a place at home. So some naive part of you yearns to return to that sense of solace.

We all do it, at some level—whether we've been married three months or three decades. We retreat to the kind of ice cream we liked as a kid or to a photo album that reminds us we were once safe and sound. Regression is a common coping strategy for dealing with conflict in marriage. Of course, there are dozens of others. And of course, there are better ways to handle the inevitable tension of conflict that arises between every normal couple.

The following is offered to help transcend the fallout that too often attends a married fight. We begin with an insight that sets the stage for a new attitude about conflict and follow it up with some of the most effective tips for "fighting fair."

One note before we go on: "Fighting" is a negative term for most people, implying winning and losing. Here, "fighting fair" it is being used as a shorthand way of talking about engaging conflict in helpful ways.

Conflict Can Be Good

One of the thoughts that went through my mind when Les and I had our first fight in that tiny kitchen was that there must be something terribly wrong with us. Loving couples don't fight, or so I thought. Turns out I couldn't have

been more wrong. The goal of marriage is not to avoid conflict. Not by a long shot. Conflict—if handled correctly—can
help build a stronger marriage. We have said it at least a
hundred times: *Conflict is the price smart couples pay for a
deepening sense of intimacy.* Without conflict, it is difficult to
peel away the superficial layers of a relationship and discover who we really are. When Ruth Graham was asked if she
and her famous husband, Billy, ever fight, she said, "I hope
so. Otherwise we would have no differences, and life would
be pretty boring."

Consider the reasons for marital spats. First of all, people
are not perfect and neither is the world we live in. While it
makes logical sense that there are no perfect marriages, many
of us still expect our marriage to be different. This expectation
alone is enough to set off countless conflicts. Another factor
that adds fuel to the fire of marital fights is the human ten-
dency to resist compromise. Every day, couples run up against
desires, big and small, that collide with each other. For example, a husband wants to work overtime to acquire enough
money to make a down payment on a house, while the wife
would rather sacrifice the savings and spend more time together at home. There is no real right or wrong side in this
scenario. Both partners have a good point, but a compromise
is needed if they are ever going to resolve it. Yet for most people, compromise is difficult, and conflict is thus inevitable.

We could go on listing reasons for turbulence in marriage. Still, no matter how deeply a man and woman love
each other, they *will* encounter conflict. It is a natural com-
ponent of every healthy marriage. So we shouldn't bury differences. Instead, view them as a potential source for culti-
vating a deeper sense of intimacy.

Walking in Other Shoes

The best way to avoid stepping on our mate's toes is to
put ourselves in his or her shoes. That's empathy—to see the
world from the partner's perspective.

Several years ago, I (Les) was conducting training seminars for elementary school teachers. To help them better understand the world of a third grader, I gave them the assignment of walking through their classroom on their knees. "I always assumed students were viewing the classroom as I was," said one teacher after completing the exercise. "It looks so different from their perspective."

We make the same error in marriage when we assume we know what our spouse is experiencing. We don't. Everyone interprets life from a composite of unique insights and perceptions. Life looks different for our spouse than it does for us, yet we tend to assume that he or she sees life as we see it. Only after entering the other's world with our heart and our head, however, can we accurately understand his or her perspective. To look at life through the same lens means asking two questions: (1) What does this situation, problem, or event look or feel like from my partner's perspective? (2) How is his or her perception different from mine?

Empathy always involves risk, so be forewarned. Accurately understanding our partner's hurts and hopes will change us. Once we consciously feel his or her feelings and understand his or her perspective, we will see the world differently. In the majority of cases, empathy is enough to bring a particular marital conflict to a screeching halt. It sets the stage for two simple words: "I'm sorry."

Apology

Apologies keep life oiled when the bearings begin to wear. A graceful apology is a curtsy to civility, a gesture that helps crowded citizens put up with each other, a modest bow to keep hassles within tolerable bounds. Within a marriage, an apology that is sincere can be a powerful tool for resolving issues and strengthening the relationship.

Sometimes apologizing is perfectly straightforward. When one partner blows it, and the offense is minor (maybe one of them forgets to put gas in the car), a graceful apology is all it takes for the incident to be dropped. At other times, an apology can be surprisingly complicated.

Like lots of couples, one husband and wife we worked with would regularly short-circuit their arguments with hasty apologies. "I said I was sorry for what I did," one of them would say. "Now why can't you forget about it and move on?"

This form of apology is really a tool of manipulation. It is a way of getting off the hook and avoiding the real issue. What's worse, a premature apology blocks real change. One husband snapped at his wife at a dinner party. Later, he said, "I'm sorry, but look, you have to understand that I've been under a lot of stress lately." The husband was avoiding responsibility for his insensitive behavior. What his wife needed to hear was, "I'm sorry. It isn't right to lash out at you when I'm stressed." This would have told the wife that her husband understood he had hurt her and would try not to do it again.

True apologies in marriage can only happen when partners come to understand accountability. This is another way of saying that each of us must take responsibility for our own behavior, acknowledge our partner's point of view, and at times own up to things about ourselves we don't like. Finally, it may mean making changes. "I had to swallow my pride and admit to something unlikable about myself," one husband told us. "But once I did, I started changing."

All couples need a healing mechanism, a way to turn a new page in marriage. Knowing how and when to say "I'm sorry" can make a big difference. We can ask ourselves these questions: When and how do we apologize? Does one of us apologize more than the other? Do we use apologies to short-circuit or cover up issues?

A sincere apology will leave a relieved sense of the air being cleared and a renewed closeness.

Not Whether We Fight but How We Fight

Repressed conflict has a high rate of resurrection. If something is bothering us, it is always best to put it out on the table and discuss it. What matters next is how we handle the conflict. Here are the experts' tips for learning to "fight fair."

First, when experiencing tension in the relationship, *plan a peace conference.* Don't ignore the conflict, hoping it will disappear. Set a mutually agreeable "appointment" time to discuss what's troublesome. This takes initiative, but it is critically important to schedule a face-to-face meeting to resolve conflict in a relationship.

Next, *cultivate a win-win attitude.* In other words, seek to understand the other's perspective before trying to "prove your case." Too many spouses become instant attorneys when it comes to marital conflict, convincing an invisible jury that they have been treated unjustly and that their partner should be found guilty. Don't fall for this fallacy. Instead, try to see the world from his or her perspective. In "fighting fair," the point is not to prove the partner wrong and win; the goal is to understand one another so both win.

This leads to another tip: *Attack the problem, not the person.* No one is going to change a spouse through arguing. Our natural impulse during conflict is to defend and protect our position, not to accommodate the other person, even when it's our spouse. If we accuse our spouse of always making us late, he or she is probably not going to say, "Oh, you're right. I'll be different from now on." He or she is more likely to tell us that we only make it worse by pressuring him or her. Or that we are too impatient. Or a hundred other reasons why he or she is not at fault. We will be far more productive if we focus on the problem of being late and work together, as a team, to devise a way of avoiding it. In other words, separate the problem from the person.

Conclusion

To sum up the idea of "fighting fair," we must be cooperative. We must be willing to flex and yield to our partner. Scripture says, "Wisdom . . . is peace-loving and courteous. It allows discussion and is willing to yield to others; it is full of mercy and good deeds. It is wholehearted and straight forward and sincere" (James 3:17, TLB). If we decide to have a cooperative attitude with our partner, we will save ourselves and our marriage a lot of unnecessary grief. And we will have found the secret to "fighting fair."

Scripture Cited: James 3:17

About the Authors: Drs. Leslie and Les Parrot are codirectors of the Center for Relationship Development at Seattle Pacific University, <http://www.realrelationships.com/>. They are the authors of *Saving Your Marriage Before It Starts, Becoming Soul Mates,* and *When Bad Things Happen to Good Marriages.*

CHAPTER 9

TURMOIL IN THE FAMILY

by CHERYL GOCHNAUER

MY FAVORITE PICTURE of my older daughter was snapped when she was five months old. Her beautiful eyes, full of unguarded trust and admiration, gaze innocently at me, her beloved mommy.

In photos taken only a couple of months later, I can spot a definite glint in those same eyes, an ornery promise of things to come.

Some might say she inherited that rebelliousness from me, but I resist that notion since her younger sister didn't get "the glint" until she was almost 10. Even then, a simple disapproving look could reduce Little Sis to tears and promises of being good.

Same genes, same environment. I don't care what the nature-or-nurture pundits say—freewill rules!

My parents were big believers in the *environment* theory. Dad, who really was an army drill sergeant, ran our home like his own private regiment. Maintaining strict discipline with a no-nonsense attitude, his homebound "troops" knew better than to question his word. And I didn't, at least not verbally. (I did hear, "Wipe that look off your face!" pretty regularly, however.)

When I finally stood up to him the summer I turned 18, our conversation was punctuated with a slamming door and 10-month silence.

For those playing at home, this is a model of how *not* to handle conflict between parents and children.

Look at Me When I'm Talking to You

My daughter may have a glint, but when I take an honest look at myself, I have to admit that it is nothing compared to my intense glare. I am relatively slow to anger (score one for biblical living!), but once lit, the resulting firestorm can level a room. As an added bonus, I am a writer, which means my verbal repertoire is extensive. When ratcheted up to full capacity, I have the ability to decimate my daughters in less than a minute.

It's not a gift I am proud of, and I am horrified to think that I could easily pass this dubious quality on to my children. I am determined to learn and implement more diplomatic ways of working through disagreements so that doesn't happen.

As we see throughout this book, life offers a variety of conflict situations for us to resolve. The interaction between parent and child is unique, however. When we clash with a coworker, a neighbor, or even a spouse, we are standing toe to toe with someone whose core attitudes and beliefs were set before we met them. When we spar with our offspring, we are arguing with individuals whose convictions were directly influenced from Day One by *us*.

With that in mind, I believe we can sidestep a lot of heartache if we remember three unshakable truths:
- You reap what you sow.
- The apple doesn't fall far from the tree.
- Train up a child in the way he or she should go, or you'll be sorry.

Author Ken Sande identifies potential idols ruling parents' hearts, including one that rings particularly true with me: "a consuming desire for respect, appreciation, control, convenience, or, to put it in simple terms, peace and quiet."[1]

Ah, peace and quiet. As I enter my 40s, I can look back and see my life break into two distinct eras: B.C. and A.D.— Before Children and After Delivery.

Respect:
- B.C.: "Congratulations. You've been promoted."

- A.D.: "Awesome, Mom. You made it to level 12 on that video game."

Appreciation:

- B.C.: "Thanks for dinner, Babe. It was delicious."
- A.D.: "Looks good, but I'm late for soccer practice. Bye!"

Control:

- B.C.: "I'm going to finish my project, run my errands, relax in the Jacuzzi, and enjoy my favorite meal."
- A.D.: None. Whether baby or teen, at any given moment, they may simply say, "You can forget about your schedule, because I'm going to fuss all day for no good reason, just because I can."

Convenience:

- B.C.: "I can leave the house in five minutes."
- A.D.: "I'll grab the diaper bag, formula, and car seat. You get the playpen, high chair, and change of clothes." Or later, "She'll be awhile. After all, one of her friends might see her at the gas station."

Since delivery, even peace and quiet is suspect. "Honey, have you seen the kids?"

Children have many of the same basic desires we do, though we likely differ in our definitions of respect, appreciation, control, and convenience. For instance, my teen thinks peace and quiet means headphones blaring dc talk as she speed-reads the most recent *Left Behind* installment with the TV on. (I can choose to view her as insane or a classic multi-tasker.)

Of course, I can look in the rearview mirror and spot *my* mom frowning at my youthful selection of clothes, music, and friends. What goes around comes around, as they say.

When these cultures clash, passive resistance or browbeating the other person until they go belly-up simply won't work. As with marital discord, unresolved parent-child conflict provides no safe zone, no haven in which to hide. Warring parties are literally in this together. If they don't learn to use conflict as a tool instead of a weapon, the resulting battles will plunge the entire household into chaos.

That Was Then, This Is Now

Recognizing that differences of opinion are a normal part of life is a critical part of constructive conflict. It's illuminating to examine the behavior of family members, based on their formative experiences.[2] For instance, my dad, the oldest of nine children, was born in the 1930s and endured both the Great Depression and the responsibility of helping raise his siblings while his father fought overseas. Considering his background, it is not surprising that Daddy held his own three kids on a tight leash.

I, on the other hand, grew up in the '60s and '70s—a time defined by social revolution, new freedoms, and a shifting moral climate. In that "let it all hang out" setting, I would probably have responded positively if my father had chosen to share his feelings about why he felt and acted the way he did. Unfortunately, his authoritarian "because I said so" and my philosophical "if it feels good, do it" didn't gel very well. So, our moments of heart-to-heart conversation were rather limited.

Now I find myself parenting products of the New Millennium, and it is as challenging as anything my mom and dad faced. The "I am OK; you're OK" vine seeded in America 30 years ago now chokes our culture with moral ambiguity. Raising my children in the church helps temper rampant false teaching, but insidious influence elsewhere is still felt. I must be constantly vigilant to keep ahead of the lies, and such caution naturally leads to battles on the home front.

When I stay tuned to God's voice, the result is productive conflict, based in love. As I tell my girls, if their dad and I didn't love them, we wouldn't care enough to oppose behavior we know will hurt them.

They roll their eyes at this point, of course, but they'll thank us for it later (I hope).

Because I Said So

You've probably heard the saying, "Presentation is everything." It is a wise parent who realizes the subtle but vital difference between discipline and punishment, and who chooses to use humor to ease tension, instead of sarcasm. Proverbs 25:11 says, "A word aptly spoken is like apples of gold in settings of silver." Along the same vein, a word sharply spoken is like a worm in that same apple. When our kids do something that punches our hot button, we should pause a moment, take a breath, then say something like:

- "That outfit isn't appropriate for this occasion" instead of "You look like a tramp."
- "You don't want to put damaging images in your brain you can't get out" rather than "I don't give a rip if everyone else is going to 'Texas Chainsaw Massacre XVI'; you're not going!"
- "Explain to me why you're upset" in place of "Wipe that look off your face." (Shades of my father!)

The generation gap is alive and kicking, but isn't necessarily something to be feared. Each member of the family holds a vital part, with a God-given role to play. And the Bible offers solid advice for working through conflict between parents and children, both while the kids are at home and once they're living on their own.

The second scenario is important, because parent-child conflict doesn't automatically disappear at graduation. The catalysts for conflict may change (inappropriate comments about where they live, what job they take, how they raise their kids), but the potential for generational head-butting still remains.

As a society, we tend to think of ourselves as free of our parents once we leave home. Yet, there is no expiration date stamped on the commandment to honor our fathers and mothers; it is a life-long commitment. However, this commandment is not without its reward. "'Honor your father and mother'—which is the first commandment with a promise—'that it may go well with you and that you may enjoy long life on the earth'" (Ephesians 6:2-3).

Believe it or not, parents may actually have something worthwhile to say. "Listen, my son, to your father's instruction and do not forsake your mother's teaching. They will be a garland to grace your head and a chain to adorn your neck" (Proverbs 1:8-9). Before dismissing criticism from our parents, we should listen carefully to their words. Maybe the message wasn't presented as carefully or as kindly as we would have liked, but does it ring true? In any case, the way we react will either ease or aggravate the conflict because "a gentle answer turns away wrath, but a harsh word stirs up anger" (Proverbs 15:1).

Working through problems with our parents as adults can give us a renewed appreciation of our own youngsters. Christian moms and dads are quick to point out Colossians 3:20, "Obey your parents in everything, for this pleases the Lord" but tend to ignore the next line, "Fathers [and mothers!], do not embitter your children, or they will become discouraged" (v. 21).

We should offer our children a measure of the same respect we desire, based upon their ages. While "because I said so" may be appropriate when dealing with a toddler, it's less effective with older children—and a worthless stance to take with teens. Resolving conflicts is an ongoing part of parenting, and we have to be ready to flex on the fly. It's challenging, no doubt. No one said raising kids was easy. In fact, Dr. James Dobson pegged it perfectly when he entitled one of his books, *Parenting Isn't for Cowards*. Nevertheless, there are few things in this life as rewarding.

Every conflict is an opportunity for growth, for both the parent and the child. The key is making the most of those opportunities. Each time, I make a choice. Will I unleash the firestorm or ease the situation through levelheaded discussion? Will I respect my child or tune him or her out? Am I God's vessel or a clanging cymbal? (see 1 Corinthians 13:1).

Ask a roomful of parents whether they love their children and every head will nod. Then ask whether they love them biblically, as in 1 Corinthians 13:4-8).

Love is patient, love is kind. "I've HAD it with you kids!"

It does not envy. "You don't know how good you've got it; I never had anything like that when I was growing up."

It does not boast, it is not proud. "You'll never be better than the old man."

It is not rude, it is not self-seeking. "Get that gunk off your face before the neighbors see you."

It is not easily angered. "I said NO!"

It keeps no record of wrongs. "I can always depend on you to mess things up."

Love does not delight in evil but rejoices with the truth. "I told you this would happen. Now you'll get what's coming to you."

It always protects. "I'm through with you."

. . . always trusts. "I don't believe you."

. . . always hopes. "You'll never amount to anything."

. . . always perseveres. "I give up."

Love never fails. "Do what you want; I don't care anymore."

We can respond better. And with God's help, we will.

As for Me and My House

It amazes me how truly inspiring the Bible is. Its most recent books were written long before the greatest of our grandparents were born, yet its advice on conflict management is as timely as yesterday's newspaper—and more applicable. Throughout Scripture, we see depictions of conflict between parents and children: the redemptive story of the lost son (Luke 15:11-32); the ill-fated rebellion of Absalom against his father, King David (2 Samuel 13—19); even the irritation of Mary with 12-year-old Jesus, who stayed behind in Jerusalem to teach while the rest of His family unknowingly headed home without Him (Luke 2:41-52).

God forms each of us as one-of-a-kind individuals, endowed with tailor-made gifts and personalities. He's a multi-faceted God who creates multifaceted people. We are complex creatures, and even when pulled from the same gene pool, completely unique.

I suspect one reason parent-child conflict can be so excruciating is because we share the same genes. I know that since giving birth, all my senses are sharper, for better or worse. Just ask any new mom riding home from the hospital in the family car. Bad drivers are no longer simply irritating. Now they are homicidal maniacs out to hurt our babies. They all need to be locked up!

Resist the hormones, and encourage your children (especially preteens and teens) to do the same. Conflict within families is natural and to be expected, as we each follow—and sometimes, stumble—along the path God has set before us. The challenge is to learn to handle these growing pains constructively, as a team.

I will try to keep this in mind the next time I spot that glint in my daughters' eyes.

Notes:

1. *Peacemaking for Families: A Biblical Guide to Managing Conflict in Your Home* (Wheaton, Ill.: Tyndale House Publishers, 2002), 135.

2. Dr. Rick and Kathy Hicks provide an excellent guide to empathizing with various age-groups in their book, *Boomers, Xers, and Other Strangers: Understanding the Generational Differences That Divide Us* (Tyndale House Publishers, 1999). The Hickses outline societal trends and mores in the United States from the 1920s through the present, providing interesting insights as to why the different generations, as a whole, behave the way they do.

Scriptures Cited: 2 Samuel 13—19; Proverbs 1:8-9; 15:1; 25:11; Luke 2:41-52; 15:11-32; 1 Corinthians 13:1, 4-8; Ephesians 6:2-3; Colossians 3:20-21

About the Author: Cheryl Gochnauer is a freelance writer from Lee's Summit, Missouri. She also is the founder of a web site for stay-at-home parents, <http://www.gospelcom.net/homebodies/>.

CHAPTER 10

A CHRISTIAN PERSPECTIVE

by RANDY T. HODGES

WHAT KEN DOES HAS to be one of the least desirable jobs available. He works on the bomb squad. Bombs—volatile, explosive, unpredictable, and highly dangerous! Who would volunteer to work on the bomb squad? The stress is horrendous. The margin for error is miniscule. On most jobs, when you make a mistake, you correct it and move on. On the bomb squad, make a mistake, and it may be your last! Could there be a more intense or dangerous job?

Talking with Ken, I learned something fascinating. When attempting to defuse a bomb, squad members are taught never to turn their backs on the explosive device.

At first, I thought he was joking. I understand the wisdom in facing down a strange dog, but a bomb? That certainly sounded peculiar. As a matter of fact, the natural reaction of most of us would be to turn away from an explosive and run—*fast.* Still, Ken's explanation of why bomb handlers do not turn their backs helps. Their protective gear is specially designed to protect the front of the bomb handler. The protective helmet and mask shield the face, while the explosion-resistant body armor and padding protect the front of the handler's torso. When the bomb expert turns his or her back, the gear ceases to protect. He or she is exposed and more vulnerable. Fascinating!

Trying to resolve conflict can resemble defusing a bomb. Like working with an unstable device, conflict can be volatile. Like handling explosives, trying to manage conflict can be unpredictable. When conflict arises, natural emotional responses often erupt, making *what we feel* seem much more intense and real. We may *feel* attacked when no attack is intended. We may *feel* unappreciated when nothing could be farther from the truth. We may *feel* we're being treated unfairly when, in reality, we ourselves are the ones being unjust. Just like handling a bomb, trying to resolve conflict can be volatile and dangerous.

Our Purpose

In this chapter, we are exploring how we, as Christians, can handle conflict in a God-honoring way. We will seek to provide basic help to enable us to work toward resolving the conflicts that we face without forsaking our commitment to God or our witness for Him.

It's true that Christians can (and sometimes do) handle conflict just like those who don't know Christ. Resorting to basic human tendencies, too often believers act no differently than unbelievers. Letting anger and frustration take over, it's too common for Christians to resort to retaliation, character assassination, or a feigned denial of the problem.

However as Christians, when we react like those who don't know Christ, we can't possibly please God. Jesus makes it clear that God blesses peacemakers. Ken Sande has it right. "As people reconciled to God by the death and resurrection of Jesus Christ, we believe that we are called to respond to conflict in a way that is remarkably different from the way the world deals with conflict."[1]

Scripture makes it clear that for those of us who claim Christ as our Lord, we are indeed to handle ourselves differently than those who don't know Jesus. To please and honor God, our response to conflict must be different. Our response must be spiritually mature and responsible. Scripture offers us help in knowing how to carry out this challenging assignment. Handling conflict in a way that is genuinely Christian may not come naturally, but with God's help, it can be done.

Ten Ways to Handle Conflict in a God-Pleasing Way

1. We can draw near to God, committing ourselves to do what He directs.

It's easy to get to the end of our understanding and wisdom. It's impossible to get to the end of God's. Since our goal is to handle conflict in a way that pleases Him, we are wise to draw closer to Him and His guidance. Hebrews 10:19-25 suggests five things we can do to draw near to God:

- *To get closer to God, we can intensify our prayer life.*

There is no substitute for talking with God when we need strength, wisdom, and guidance. When Jesus faced Calvary, He went to the Father repeatedly, committing and recommitting himself to do just what God desired. If Jesus needed that communion in prayer, we need it even more.

- *We can refuse to "play games" when we talk with God, pretending everything is wonderful when it is not.*

Some find it easy to lapse into telling God whatever they think He wants to hear. It's as if they somehow believe that if they tell Him everything is great, He will believe their conflict does not exist. Yet, playing this kind of game with God does not help us with our challenge.

We have the privilege of talking with God about our problems—our real problems. (Take my word for it, there's nothing you can tell Him that He's never heard before.) And in admitting what we are facing, we find God to be merciful and understanding. He's a source of great strength and of wise guidance. He will reveal a solution to us if we are willing to discuss our problem with Him.

- *To draw closer to God, we can correct our own faults before criticizing and condemning those we see in others.*

Jesus said it this way: "First take the plank out of your own eye, and then you will see clearly to remove the speck from your brother's eye" (Matthew 7:5).

Ken Sande writes, "Self-examination is especially important when we are involved in a dispute. Until we have dealt with our faults, it will be difficult to help others see how

they have contributed to a dispute. But once we have con-
fessed our wrongs and repaired any damage we have done,
others will often be encouraged to follow our example and
listen to our words."[2]

- *Seek to let the love of God in Christ Jesus live in us and flow
  through us.*

Scripture says, "Love never fails" (1 Corinthians 13:8). If
in going to God we can become channels for passing along
His love, we will more effectively handle the conflict we face
in a God-honoring way.

- *To get closer to God, stay connected with other believers in
  the church for mutual support and encouragement.*

We really do need one another! God places us with other
believers to help us. When conflict erupts, some act like a
dropped bag of marbles—they roll off in every possible direction. Nevertheless, in the Body of Christ, we are called to
respond more like a bunch of grapes. Since a common vine,
Jesus Christ, unites us, we don't need to scatter. Instead, we
can stay together. And through that vine, we can share nour-
ishment, aims, and the same end. In times of difficulty, we
need the love and perspective of those who are also connected with Christ. To get closer to Him, we can draw closer to
His Body, the Church.

   2. *We can refuse to let our natural impulses rule us by staying
self-controlled.*

You've probably see a big, heavy steam engine, the kind
once used on the farm to generate power. A long belt attached to the old-fashioned steam engine connected it to a
thresher or maybe a saw, transferring power as needed. On
the top of the steam engine, an intriguing little device spins,
looking more like a part of a toy than a powerful machine.
It's the governor. The governor regulates the power so the
engine will not roar out of control.

First Thessalonians 5:8 says, "Let us be self-controlled,
putting on faith and love as a breastplate, and the hope of
salvation as a helmet."

A wise person said it well: "Self-control is the ability to keep cool while someone is making it hot for you."[3] Self-control is the governor that helps keep little conflicts from becoming major wars.

3. We can take the initiative to resolve the problem.

Here's what Jesus says in Matthew 5:23-24, "If you are offering your gift at the altar and there remember that your brother has something against you, leave your gift there in front of the altar. First go and be reconciled to your brother; then come and offer your gift."

Did you get that? If we realize that anyone has something against us, we are to go to that person and try to work things out. We are to take the first step. This flies in the face of what most would naturally do. "If he has a problem, he can come to me" is a more common attitude.

If Jesus said to go and make things right if we are upset with someone, I could understand that. However, Christ raises the bar on personal responsibility when He says if "your brother has something against you," then you go and be reconciled. Jesus hands the responsibility to us to take the first step in making peace with those around us.

Obviously, Jesus takes peace seriously.

4. We can try to defuse the emotion from the situation by clearly defining the root cause of the problem.

To be effective as peacemakers, we need to do another thing that is unnatural. We need to defuse the emotion from the conflict. To do so, it can be helpful to carefully write out in clear and simple words the root cause of the conflict. It may take several attempts to get it right. Without attacking the character of those with whom you have difficulty, try to precisely identify the root cause of the issue.

Though cumbersome, this process may provide significant insight by working with the problem on paper in a less emotionally charged way. It may even provide a key to resolving the problem.

5. We can identify what legitimately can be done to resolve the conflict.

There are probably some wise things we can do to move toward peace. Maybe there's a phone call we need to make. It might be a note we should write. Perhaps there's a kind word to speak. Or, it may be that we need to stop repeating the injustice of our situation to every person we meet.

The more often we rehearse any difficult situation, the more emotionally charged we become. We can talk ourselves into being upset. Sometimes, just being quiet and letting the situation cool off is very wise. In some cases, all that may be needed is closing our mouth.

Another helpful thing we can do that can lead to resolution is simply to listen. Sometimes, people respond better just knowing that they have been heard.

6. *We can try to better understand the perspective of those with whom we are in conflict.*

The middle-aged man sat on the bus mindlessly staring at nothing, as his three younger children bounced off the walls. The other riders grew increasingly annoyed as the unruly children created havoc with no response from their father. Frustration escalated as the father sat silently, seemingly oblivious to their wild behavior.

One passenger, angered after nearly being hit by a flying object, finally had enough. He approached the father, saying, "Sir, could you please control your children?"

The father looked up and mumbled, "Oh, yeah . . . I guess I should . . . I'm sorry. We're just coming from the hospital. Their mother just passed away. I guess I'm not paying much attention."

When the irate passenger learned what was really taking place, his anger and frustration melted. In place of anger, sympathy and compassion flowed. It would for anyone knowing the rest of the story.

7. *We can search for a solution that will meet both their needs and ours.*

It is wise to seek solutions that are beneficial to everyone. When involved in any conflict, it is easy to dig in, trying to defend our own interests. Still, rather than competition, co-operation often works better.

Philippians 2:4 says, "Look not only to your own interests, but also to the interests of others."

On an out-of-town trip, we filled the car with gasoline. Continuing down the road, our car soon began to hesitate, sputter, and die. The nearest mechanic confirmed the problem—contaminated gasoline had clogged the fuel lines and filters.

In contacting the station where the bad fuel had been purchased, I got little cooperation in getting my car repaired. The manager's initial response was, "We're not responsible. It's your problem."

I decided to try another approach. I called again and this time said, "Look, I have no intention of pursuing legal action. I'm trying to be a person of honor and to treat you as the same. Could we work together to find a solution that would be agreeable to both of us?"

From that point on, it was like I was dealing with a different person. The previously uncooperative manager became helpful. Soon we came to an agreement—fair to both of us—that resolved the problem.

When a solution lets both sides win, both sides win!

8. We can refuse to allow our heart and attitude to be poisoned by bitterness.

"Bitterness is like drinking poison and waiting for the other person to die."[4]

If anyone feels entitled to be bitter, there's a good chance Terry Anderson has more reasons. As the Associated Press's chief Middle East correspondent, he experienced a needless hell no one should have to endure.

In March of 1985, Shiite Muslims kidnapped him in Beirut, Lebanon. Day after day, Anderson was held hostage, imprisoned though having broken no laws. Separated from his family, his friends, his home, his comforts, he lost all that was dear to him. His ordeal went on for years. Finally, as the last American hostage released, Anderson returned to freedom. His captivity had lasted nearly seven years.

From 1985 to 1992, Anderson lost a huge part of his life he could never recover. If anyone has a good reason to be bitter, Anderson was a prime candidate.

Here's what Terry Anderson said in his first public speaking appearance after being released. "I have no room for hate, I have no time for it. My hating them is not going to hurt them an ounce; it's only going to hurt me."[5]

Terry Anderson knew it, and so should we: Conflict can be the door through which bitterness enters our heart. Never drink the poison of bitterness.

9. *If we do not immediately succeed, we can keep trying, realizing that not every conflict can be quickly resolved.*

Many will respond to Scripture's peacemaking principles. However, we may encounter those who refuse to be reconciled no matter what we do. Sometimes these folks will continue to intentionally mistreat us. It may be tempting, after trying to respond in a God-pleasing way, to give up and give in to the urge to strike back. Nevertheless, Jesus calls us to a different response: "But I tell you who hear me: Love your enemies, do good to those who hate you, bless those who curse you, pray for those who mistreat you. . . . love your enemies, do good to them. . . . Then your reward will be great, and you will be sons of the Most High, because he is kind to the ungrateful and wicked. Be merciful, just as your Father is merciful" (Luke 6:27-28, 35-36).

A legend pictures an aged gentleman meditating on the bank of a rising river. Just beyond the water's edge, he spots a scorpion trapped on the roots of a tree. Feeling compassion, the man reaches out to rescue the scorpion from the rising water, but each time he reaches out, the scorpion strikes at him.

A nearby observer speaks up. "It's just a scorpion. Why bother?"

The gentleman replies, "Because it's the scorpion's nature to strike is no reason for me to disregard my nature to help."

10. If no immediate resolution takes place, we can stay committed to loving obedience.

The essence of living a holy lifestyle is loving God with all our hearts and our neighbors as ourselves—even that cantankerous neighbor whose petty complaints keep the whole block upset.

Martin Luther King Jr. knew conflict. His peaceful resistance tactics in the Civil Rights Movement of the 1960s helped us learn to accept others. King once said, "I have decided to stick with love. Hate is too great a burden to bear."[6]

Conclusion

Every time we are confronted with conflict, we face a decision. As Christians, it's vital that we realize the significance of the choice we make.

When we come upon the fires of contention, it is as if we carry a bucket in each hand. One bucket is filled with gasoline. When a quarrel or a misunderstanding occurs, we can pour gasoline on the fire and watch it grow. Some seem to enjoy seeing how big they can make the flames of conflict erupt. We can promote discord by fanning the flames of disunity, disagreement, and disharmony. But we cannot fan those flames and still please our Lord.

Our other bucket is filled with water. If we will, we can douse the flames of conflict, making them smaller, and maybe even extinguishing them completely. We can be peacemakers. When we choose this godly task, our Lord is very pleased, God is glorified, and we will find inner joy and peace in our souls.

Jesus said, "Blessed are the peacemakers, for they will be called sons of God" (Matthew 5:9).

Which bucket will we use?

Notes:

1. Ken Sande, *The Peacemaker: A Biblical Guide to Resolving Personal Conflict* (Grand Rapids: Baker Book House, 1997), 235.

2. Sande, 91.

3. *Draper's Quotations for the Christian World,* 9961.

4. Ron McManus, *Leadership,* Spring 2000, 73.

5. *The Wichita Eagle,* May 5, 1992.

6. *Draper's,* 7182.

Scriptures Cited: Matthew 5:9, 23-24; 7:5; Luke 6:27-28, 35-36; 1 Corinthians 13:8; Philippians 2:4; 1 Thessalonians 5:8; Hebrews 10:19-25

About the Author: Dr. Randy Hodges is senior pastor of the Maysville Church of the Nazarene, Maysville, Kentucky.

CHAPTER 11

FAILURES IN FRIENDSHIPS

by JON JOHNSTON

SEVERAL YEARS AGO a group of Palestinian and Israeli youth were airlifted to a United States retreat environment, far from the rancorous voices in their countries. Upon arrival, they were encouraged to simply relax, have fun together, and let things take their natural course.

What followed warmed their sponsors' hearts. Relationships took root that produced beautiful blossoms of friendship. As a welcome bonus, brutal stereotypes began to vanish like morning fog. Intimacies were shared; promises were made; even consensus was calmly reached on strategies for peace.

Then came that final day. Tearful good-byes and heartfelt intentions to keep in touch were expressed. Vastly dissimilar youth had done it—proven their bigoted warlord leaders dead wrong. These young people had surmounted obstacles to converge into an authentic friendship community.

Reabsorption into Chaos

Upon their return, a sea of beckoning fingers lured these bright youth in many directions. Nevertheless, they made time to periodically write, call, and even visit one another. Most important, they retained great memories of, and warm feelings for, their friends "on the other side."

Then things suddenly changed. The *infitada* (territorial uprisings in the West Bank and Gaza Strip) began its reign of terror. Rocks sailed at tanks. Bombs exploded in crowded business districts. Victors and victims spewed vows of vengeance. The sword of violence divided the Holy Land into two warring camps. In sociological terms, its two cultures engaged in "relationship regression"—backpedaling from *assimilation* (cooperation with) to *accommodation* (toleration for) to *accostation* (militancy against).

In the midst of this melee, a TV network decided to do a where-are-they-now special on the campers. Had their cross-cultural friendships intensified, neutralized, or gone sour? Would they consider making contact? Had their attitudes remained open and positive?

To the chagrin of reporters, these close chums of yester-year—themselves now overdosed on cultural venom—began lashing out at their counterparts with little restraint. Saddest of all, it was clear that they even judged one another completely guilty by association.

Willing to resume contact with one another? No longer. Feelings of mutuality had dissipated as rapidly as the smoke residue of a homicidal bomb.

One responder's declaration captured the deep sentiment. He was asked, "What if you spotted your camp friend approaching your settlement? Would you rush to embrace or protect him? Or would you run and hide, to not be publicly associated with him?"

Steely-eyed and unflinching, the youth replied, "I'd immediately grab my gun and shoot him dead!"

"Why?"

"Because I'd assume he was there to kill us."

As illustrated in this example, just as sure as friendships can form and yield pleasure, they can cease and produce torment. That's why it's worthwhile to comprehend the dynamics and impact of friendship conflict. More is involved than we might think. A lot more. As Samuel Butler wrote a long time ago, "Friendship is like money, easier made than kept."

When Friendships Do a "Deep Six"

Many friendships perish from neglect, though it amazes

me how many dormant friendships are instantly quickened by the slightest overtures of contact.

Other friendships don't simply fizzle-out—they suddenly explode. And the sequence of events often follows this four-stage pattern:

1. A buildup ("gunnysacking") of resentment accumulates, having not been continuously, methodically processed.

2. When the "sack" reaches saturation point, a flash-point issue surfaces, one containing lots of "rigor" (defined as "that something present when something big is at stake"). The precipitant can be as major as a lost job or as trivial as an undercooked egg. The issue isn't what is important. Rather, it's the significance attached to it, and the backlog of unprocessed, unresolved grievance that churns within.

3. Damage assessment inventory takes place. Two questions get asked: "How much have all involved been hurt?" And "What havoc and injury is *perceived* by others?"

4. The response strategy is chosen, which is usually modified as things play out. Typically, it is more retaliatory and self-protective at first, but less so as the intensity wanes.

You might ask, doesn't this process characterize most interpersonal conflicts, friendship-based or otherwise? No doubt. Still, there is something about friendship skirmishes that greatly increases the potential for prolonged (even irreparable) damage.

To understand this fact more fully, let's take a close look at the basic nature of friendship.

When People Bond

There are four kinds of people we continuously encounter on this planet.

- *Distant.* Folks who feel detached or alienated from and apathetic toward us. We don't even appear on their "radar screens."

- *Different.* People who sense estrangement from us, and

we from them, by virtue of our contrasting features or life experiences.

- *Defiant.* Individuals who detest what we are and stand for and, as a result, resist our overtures—regardless how noble.

- *Devoted.* Persons who thoroughly embrace our identity and purposes, no matter how we're perceived by others. These are our true and trusted friends—our human "teddy bears."[1]

Of these, it can be said that the last gives us the most pleasure, comfort, and affirmation. Abraham Lincoln equated having just one friend with being truly wealthy. On the flip side, those devoted to us extract the lion's share of our resources—time, possessions, energy.

Friends are persons who know us as we are, understand where we've been, accept who we have become, and still gently invite us to grow. That's why we need them—to make life worthwhile. To make it possible to put up with those other three kinds of people. To fill a gaping void in our lives. In a real sense, without our friends, life is truly incomplete.

Levels of Friendship

Of course, all friendships are not close nor intense. As we look at four types of friends in what follows, let's envision the faces of friends we have now or have had in the past.

Level One: Acquaintances[2]

These are people in our ever-changing relationships that collect in the course of daily living. People we recognize, smile at, or say hello to in the market. Those we interact with as they serve us—the dentist, gasoline attendant, and bank teller. Estimates are that we're involved with between 500 and 2,000 acquaintances each year.

Level Two: Casual Friends

Casual friends are those we see somewhat regularly,

know on a first-name basis, and meet socially on occasion. They number from 20 to 100, and their friendships may last from a few months to a lifetime.

Though important for social and economic reasons, casual friendships rarely satisfy our innermost social needs. Why? They are usually oriented toward personal gain, and thus tend to be superficial.

Level Three: Close Friends

Some casual friends become close friends, which are of three kinds:

- *associate friends:* ones who emerge from mutual participation (for example, involved in a Bible study together)
- *personal friends:* ones who remain close, regardless of time lapse or distance (for example, sorority sisters)
- *mentor friends:* ones who have guided or taught us (for example, former professor or counselor)

We have from 10 to 30 active, close friends and about the same number of inactive ones, usually from whom we're separated.

Level Four: Intimate Friends

A few of our close friends trickle into our pool of intimate friendships, of which most of us have four max. Why only four? Because they consume so much of our time, energy, and concern (and cell phone air time). To these we bare our souls, unhesitatingly revealing our deepest needs, aspirations, and secrets.

We embrace them even when they criticize us. In fact, some of us solicit their painful analysis of our ideas and performance. We feel they've earned the right to "fire away," since they're sure to be honest, keep things confidential, and always have our welfare at heart. Is it any wonder the writer of Proverbs penned, "Better is open rebuke than hidden love. Wounds from a friend can be trusted, but an enemy multiplies kisses" (27:5-6)?

We all need our special "best buddies." Comforting to us by simply being there. Always ready to participate in helpful and healthy exchange or just listen, and knowing which to do when. Conversely, our hearts are joyful when we're able to respond to them in a warm and helpful way.

However, as previously alluded to, good and close friends can experience the choppy waters of conflict. How can such idyllic, gratifying relationships go sour?

Let's try to come up with possible answers.

Friendships Are Vulnerable

The adage, "The higher the climb, the harder the fall," applies to scores of friendships that "crash and burn." In short, the high intensity of positive emotion characterizing them when they fly high morphs into negative emotion when they spiral downward. For this to occur, something perceived to be major is usually required.

- Jan and Jean were inseparable. Then a chance meeting destroyed both of their days. Why? Different opinions of the same pastor led to a major blowup, and the thick walls went up.
- Charlie and Al shared often and deeply. However, after going into business together, they clashed on their philosophy of operation. Now they've not only parted, they've countersued!
- Jim and Marge, good friends, worked professionally together on the church board. That was before the accusation of "questionable use of funds." Result: 8+ on the Richter Scale.

In all three cases, in muffled tones, bewildered bystanders could only say to one another, "Who would have thought this could have ever happened? Especially to such great friends."

What kinds of things can torpedo friendships? I'll start the list and, no doubt, you'll have ones to add.

1. *Friends can ease into an overfamiliarity that extinguishes*

respect. Jim attested to how being excessively teased on a fishing trip led to his "blowing his stack" and the subsequent cessation of a friendship.

2. Closely related, as previously mentioned, *friends can afflict one another with a "raging case of neglect."* Mary connected less with Sue, who, in turn, concluded that they must no longer be friends and refused to return Mary's calls.

3. *Friendships can be triangulated.* Others can exert enough pressure to put the kibosh on friendships. Recall our illustration of the youthful Israeli and Palestinian campers. The strident voices back home triangulated their friendships.

4. *Perception of betrayal, when so much trust is assumed, can end a friendship.* In the book, *Stuck in a Sticky World,* I cite a personal, perplexing, and heartbreaking instance related to such a perception. It has yet to reach a full resolution.

5. *One party in a friendship can decide to cease giving, or reciprocating, and start demanding.* Amanda became a proverbial "doormat" for her husband, catering to his every demand. Now, though married and still "lovers," they are no longer true friends. Why? Amanda feels thoroughly exploited.

6. *Friends can develop new priorities that clash.* Folks I know began to incessantly talk about three new obsessions: Las Vegas vacations, suing anyone for anything, and milking life savings of unsuspecting senior citizens. These combined to light the fuse of a bomb that exploded a friendship.

All six of these can cause deep and extensive damage, enough to produce relationship-severing conflicts. Furthermore, others are often impacted by collateral damage (for example, being forced to choose sides). It's potentially a lose-lose scenario for all concerned.

The big question looms: What are we to do when conflict explodes and continues to smolder between friends? Are there some tips that can make a difficult situation less so? Let's explore a few suggestions.

Picking Up the Remaining Pieces

As believers and followers of the One who responded to conflict in a perfect fashion and used it for good purposes, our approach contrasts with that of the world. How?

Rejecting their life-is-a-popularity-contest notion, Paul advises believers to be selective when choosing intimates. He realized that, in a real sense, we increasingly become like those with whom we bond.

He strongly dissuades us from being "yoked together with unbelievers" (2 Corinthians 6:14), then rhetorically asks what righteousness and wickedness, light and darkness, believer and nonbeliever have in common. Point established: Some friendships are better squelched, for they militate against our true spirituality. As an old-timer bluntly put it, "Sleeping with dogs is apt to give you fleas."

Second, contrary to the popular adage, it doesn't always take two to have conflict. Granted, two persons are required to create a positive relationship, but one can torpedo it. Thus, when we're not at fault, we must not allow guilt to consume us. God's Spirit can be trusted to sensitize us when we've erred, usually by applying the written Word to our hearts (see 2 Timothy 3:16-17). That trumps whatever Satan or anyone else may say to falsely accuse us.

Third, in the aftermath of a friendship blowup, it is imperative that we continue loving. Proverbs 17:17 declares, "A friend loves at all times." Suspensions of loving never computes for followers of the One who never hated nor retaliated. Why? His kind of love is unconditional, and relinquishes all retaliations and reprimands to God, who alone sees clearly and judges fairly.

Fourth, as followers filled with His power, we must attempt to restore shattered relationships. Jesus commands us to seek reconciliation with any person (friend or otherwise) who has sinned against us; first alone, and if no avail, in tandem with one or two other Christians (see Matthew

18:15-16). Only after these overtures are rebuffed can we, in clear conscience, terminate our efforts. But we must continue to pray.

Fifth, we who are forgiven must extend forgiveness lavishly, even when not requested nor desired. Forgiveness is often misconceptualized. It doesn't necessarily imply that we'll forget or continue schmoozing with the other party like "old times." Instead, forgiveness extracts the poison from wounds, allowing both of us to get on with our spiritual journeys. Furthermore, it positions us in an optimal place for regenerating relationships, should that ever be desired by both parties.

A Missionary Journey That Imploded

They had trailblazed effectively together, compatible in vision and spiritual fervency. Paul and Barnabas. A more solid friendship could not be perceived. Just after Paul's conversion, Barnabas had convinced the church leaders to accept this former persecutor of Christians. Paul reciprocated by making Barnabas his assistant on missionary journeys.

Yet, suddenly, a thorny issue arose that promptly and sharply divided them. Let's rewind the tape a bit to view the story (see Acts 15:36-41).

Paul invited Barnabas for an encore tour of cities they had evangelized. A journey to celebrate and check on progress being made. Barnabas agreed, but requested that they take his cousin, John Mark. This didn't set well with Paul, who vividly recalled the youth's flaking out in Pamphylia on an earlier journey. It was as if he turned to Barnabas and asked, "What is it about desertion you don't understand?"

Their disagreement was so severe that it prompted them to part company and go their separate ways—no doubt, more than a tad miffed.

Conflict between friends. Exhibit A. And both missionaries at that! If anyone ought to be immune from such squabbles, these two would seem to qualify. Paul, nurturer of young churches and Barnabas, whose very name meant "son of encouragement." Nevertheless, they fought big time!

Without glossing over or excusing this major spat, we can extract some positive features that might provide guidance for us.

First, their conflict did not result in a separation from, or blaming of, God. Both seemed to accept it as a clash of personalities or significant difference of opinion. No need to catastrophize it into more than it was, a deep disagreement between two committed believers.

Second, the combatants didn't lose a beat. Both immediately enlisted other partners—Barnabas tapped John Mark, and Paul chose Silas—and immersed themselves in ministry. As a result, their efforts were multiplied by dividing. Cyprus was added to the list of ministry targets.

Finally, though we've no record of Paul and Barnabas becoming best buddies again, Scripture implies that Paul offered John Mark his second chance. We see Paul requests Timothy to "get [John] Mark and bring him with you, because he is helpful to me in my ministry" (2 Timothy 4:11).

Friendship conflicts, though not enjoyable nor ideal, can eventually result in some good. But only if we cease playing the blame game, continue laboring in obedience, and trust God with the results.

Notes:

1. Jon Johnston, *Walls or Bridges: How to Build Relationships That Glorify God* (Grand Rapids: Baker, 1988).

2. These helpful classifications are based on gradations of lesser to greater degrees of intimacy, developed by Jerry White in his book, *Friends and Friendship: The Secrets of Drawing Closer* (Colorado Springs: Navpress, 1982).

Scriptures Cited: Proverbs 17:17; 27:5-6; Matthew 18:15-16; Acts 15:36-41; 2 Corinthians 6:14; 2 Timothy 3:16-17; 4:11

About the Author: Dr. Jon Johnston is a professor of sociology at Pepperdine University, Malibu, California.

CHAPTER 12

CONTENTION IN CHURCH

by ED ROBINSON

PASTOR KELLY CALLED and wanted to talk. I listened as she dumped her emotional frustrations and poured out her pastoral heart. She had resigned her pastorate after just one year. She'd accepted the call to the congregation, the third in a dozen years of ministry, with the understanding that they "were ready to grow" and "wanted to make some changes." Pastor Kelly's youthful demeanor and innovative style "were just what was needed."

It didn't take long for Kelly to figure out that not all the parishioners felt that way. In fact, many of the people who'd been around for a while wanted to preserve some of the traditions and practices that were a part of the church's history and personality. Some of the up-and-coming young leaders, many who'd been at the church for less than five years, were the ones who were pressing the change agenda. Battle lines were quickly formed, and Kelly and her family got caught in the crossfire. For one side, Kelly could do no wrong. For the other, she could do no right, even if her ministry depended on it (and it did!). She couldn't live up to one group's expectation and couldn't live down the other's. She was in a "no-win" situation.

Kelly and her family lost, the change faction lost, the status quo faction lost, and the whole congregation lost. The only winner was Satan, who delights in any destructive conflict. Before long, Kelly had no choice but to resign and seek another pastoral assignment far enough away to flee the rumors and wrath that accompany this kind of ugly situation.

In a different setting, another conflict occurred.

John and Mary didn't want to, but they'd put it off for too long already. Church attendance had been slipping long enough that now it was in a full-scale slide. Tithes and offerings were down, and general apathy and/or pessimism permeated the congregation. Pastor Jones was a good man with a big heart. Everyone liked him, but few valued his pastoral leadership. He couldn't lead, and somebody had to tell him.

John and Mary, both lay leaders, worried about the church's future. They worried about Pastor Jones's future as well. If the current pattern continued, both pastor and church might be dead in less than two years. How would they tell him of their concern without hurting his feelings? How could they let Pastor Jones know that even though they loved and respected him, they believed a significant change, maybe even a pastoral change, was necessary? How could they avoid being perceived as "the folks who ran the pastor out of town"?

John and Mary considered all the potential consequences of their actions and decided that the possibilities from doing nothing were far worse than whatever negative fallout might occur as a result of encouraging change. So they met with Pastor Jones and, as graciously as they knew to be, shared their concerns. Pastor Jones had suspected some dissatisfaction and was appreciative of their honesty. Nevertheless, he was hurt. What ensued was a long, hard, painful journey that ended with Pastor Jones's resignation and a demoralized church.

In yet another place, a different conflict arose.

The Greens and the Brookses are still feuding. They both knew the old adage, "Never go into a high-risk business venture with family or friends." However, they thought since they went to the same church and had been friends for years, they wouldn't succumb to the temptations others who didn't share a common spiritual commitment might. So they proceeded to invest life savings, second mortgages, and pensions in a "sure-fire" venture that didn't take very long to prove itself a dud. Accusations and allegations began to fly as freely as leaves in an autumn wind. The families stopped talking to each other and started sitting on opposite sides of the sanctuary. Mounting debts and diminishing resources ended in a declaration of insolvency. The business went bankrupt, and so did their relationship. What began in a dream ended in a court of law.

It has been a few years since the conflict and all the legalities are resolved. Yet, the whole congregation is still affected by the rift. Nobody talks about it much anymore, but everyone knows the feud and its effects are still there. Lay leadership decisions are weighed in light of the conflict. Even informal social occasions are "calculated" in light of the broken relationships. The situation is slowly but surely taking its toll on the whole church.

All three scenarios are true. I wish they weren't, but these and thousands like them occur regularly in congregations. Some are as trivial as disagreements over decaf or regular coffee, vertical or horizontal blinds in the new fellowship hall, more choruses or hymns in the morning worship service, or the "color of the new carpet in the sanctuary" conflict legendary in building committee lore. I once was in a meeting where we "discussed" for almost two hours about which brand of power lawn mower to buy for the church! We don't have to look beyond a single Sunday morning in a local congregation to find several examples. Frankly, many congregations manage the small conflicts pretty well.

However, some church conflicts are substantial. Some are grounded in theological convictions about the primary beliefs, purposes, and practices of the church. Others are embedded in broken relationships that have been fractured for so long that few in the congregation actually remember what caused the conflict in the first place, but the lingering effects are very real and run deep. Some conflicts find their center around pastoral and lay leadership. Sometimes these leadership conflicts are driven by personality differences, misunderstood expectations, or simply lack of confidence in abilities of those who are "in charge." A few church conflicts are caused by "habitual church antagonists" who move from church to church, sowing discontent, seeking power, challenging authority, and leaving a wake of havoc for pastoral and lay leaders alike. Some of these serious conflicts have resulted in wounded, hurt, demoralized and, on rare occasions, split congregations.

One would think that church, particularly a "holy" church, would be one of the places in life that would be free of conflict. With all the spiritual talk about "one Lord, one faith, one baptism" (Ephesians 4:5), "in honor preferring one another" (Romans 12:10, KJV), preserving "the unity of the Spirit in the bond of peace" (Ephesians 4:3), "obey your leaders and submit to their authority" (Hebrews 13:17), one would think that a decent, reasonably healthy church would be one place on earth where there wouldn't be conflict. One would think, but one would be wrong!

Churches are no more exempt from conflict than any strong family or loving marriage. In fact, the more active and vibrant a local church, the more likelihood of conflict, from the outside and inside. The conflicts that come from the outside arise from enemies of God who would seek to destroy the church's strength and witness in the world. The stronger the witness, the greater is the opposition and/or persecution. Conflicts from the inside are of both the trivial and substantial sort and everything in-between. If the congregation is living in obedience to God's call on their church, they are going to "ruffle some feathers" of insiders because they are going to risk doing some things that some will not like, and they'll refuse to do other things simply because "everyone else is doing it." Even when there is unanimity among the congregation to be obedient to God's mission and purposes, there will be different ideas (and disagreement) about how to accomplish them. Sometimes the practical ideas conflict even when there is agreement on the mission.

Dealing with Conflict

The question is not whether or not there will be conflict in the church. There will be. The issue is how we in the church will resolve and manage those conflicts; whether we will allow the conflict to be constructive or destructive, to unite or divide. The only absolutely bad church conflict is the unrecognized and unaddressed one. Every recognized church conflict moving toward resolution and reconciliation has the potential for good. Just like in families and personal relationships, church conflicts provide opportunities for growth.

Dealing with small conflicts can avert larger ones. If congregations will learn how to work through the little, inconsequential differences of agreement and learn to move forward together without complete unanimity of every issue that arises (for example, kind of coffee, color of carpet, menu for the brunch, type of lawn mower), then when larger issues that have greater weight and greater potential for destruction arise, people have experience and ability to work through issues in redemptive and reconciling ways. Perhaps if John, Mary, and the rest of the lay leaders had discussed with Pastor Jones some of the smaller pastoral leadership inadequacies early on in his ministry, something could have been done to adjust assignments or explore strategies for improvement.

Conflicts can provide opportunities for congregations to gain new information, new perspectives, new creativity, and even new behaviors (including better relational skills in dealing with conflict). When there is a clash of ideals, deeply grounded preferences (for example, church music), or simply the facts of a situation (for example, *is* there enough money to pay for the much-needed heating repairs?), it is best to approach the conflict systematically. Gather as much information as is helpful. Make an intentional effort to listen to others' opinions. As well as being confident that one's own views are being heard, take time to re-evaluate priorities and seek God's direction in prayer.

When things are going well, we don't often take time to engage in such focused behaviors. We're too busy making progress. Yet when crises arise, congregational leaders can either avoid the hard work, hoping the issue will resolve itself, or they can take advantage of the opportunity to gain a broader foundation and a more focused vision. Perhaps if the opposing sides in Pastor Kelly's church had done things differently . . . Taken the time to listen to each other and pray together about what God wanted for their church. Spent more time talking to each other than to everyone else about each other. Taken the opportunity to rehearse some of the heart of the conversations in the initial pastoral interview. Maybe Pastor Kelly and her family would still be at the church, and they would be moving forward with contributions from both the long-time members and the newcomers.

Conflicts have the potential for increasing a congregation's unity and bond to each other. When conflicts comes, especially from outside the church or from circumstances that are beyond the control of those involved, congregations often become stronger in their faith in God, their resolve to be faithful to God's calling and purpose for them, and committed in love to each other to see the hardship through. Strange though it may seem, persecution of Christians often results in stronger personal faith and larger congregations. Many congregations have weathered the storm of a financial crisis with a clearer sense of stewardship and a better giving record. Many congregations have suffered with a beloved member who is struggling with a fatal cancer and come to the end of that "Jericho road" with a true sense of love for God and each other that transcends the convenience of material or physical blessing. Many congregations have banded together in prayer vigils in order to turn the heart and/or mind of a civic agent who, for no apparent good reason, was standing in the way of authorizing an essential permit or certificate.

External adversity breeds cohesion, especially in churches. Image what might have happened if the Greens and the

Brookses would have used the financial adversity to strengthen their friendship rather than destroy it. Imagine what might have happened if the congregation would have seen this as an opportunity to provide financial and moral support to the families involved. It likely would not have saved a business, but it might have saved a relationship.

Conflict in the Early Church

Two of the earliest church conflicts described in the Acts of the Apostles provide an open window into ways in which conflicts can become opportunities. The New Testament church, whose birth is described in Acts 2 and whose unity is extolled as "all the believers were together and had everything in common" (v. 44), faced a conflict early in its existence that had the potential for the first church split!

Acts 6:1-7 describes an incident in which a group of Greek-speaking Christians confronted the Aramaic-speaking believers because they felt their widows weren't getting the appropriate share in the daily distribution of food. I can imagine the argument was pretty heated, with allegations of favoritism or nepotism.

The problem, simply defined, was that some in the church were being neglected. The apostles weren't making sure that what was supposed to be done was actually being done. The apostles could have ignored the problem and hoped it would go away. They could have argued that the Greeks didn't really understand the heavy weight of responsibility the apostles carried, and they should keep quiet and be happy with whatever food the Greek widows got. They could have accused the Greek-speaking believers of having unrealistic expectations for the apostles and assigning the problem of Greek widows back on the Greeks instead of relying on the whole church to address the issue. They could have given any or all of these responses (and added to the conflict), but they didn't.

They recognized that the fair and equitable distribution

of food to the widows was a problem. However, it was not favoritism, false expectation of leadership, or lack of initiative on the part of the Greeks. The problem was one of leadership and administrative structure and process. So, after seeking the guidance of the Holy Spirit, they reiterated their central mission and purpose, changed the structure, and instituted a better process.

What emerged from the conflict were stronger, more focused apostolic leaders (that is, giving attention to prayer and the ministry of the Word) and a broader, more effective lay leadership base with the gifts, graces, and time to care for the effective distribution of food. What began as a crisis ended in a stronger, more vibrant, unified church. "So the word of God spread. The number of disciples in Jerusalem increased rapidly, and a large number of priests became obedient to the faith" (v. 7). The neglect of the Greek widows was a good conflict.

Acts 15 records the interactions of the apostles and elders in Jerusalem over the question of Jewish circumcision for Gentile Christians. The conflict was primarily a theological one. In brief, as more and more Gentiles became Christians through the spread of the gospel throughout the Roman Empire, some of the Jewish Christians believed these new converts needed to abide by all the same expectations that the Jewish Christians did. That is, they needed to keep the Jewish laws, especially the one that required all males to be circumcised.

A major conflict ensued. To think that the apostles, elders, and protagonists sat around a well-decorated table, with cold water pitchers and fancy drinking glasses, politely following diplomatic protocol and waiting for their turn to speak would be far from the truth. The argument was heavy and heated. People spoke over one another and persisted until they had the privilege of everyone's ear. What is recorded in the biblical "minutes" of the council meeting was likely only a small portion of the conversation. It would be better to imagine the meeting as a free-for-all. Luke, the author of Acts, simply bundles up the verbal melee in his short description, "after much discussion" (v. 7).

This theological conflict had all the makings of a major church division every bit as great as the Protestant Reformation that would ensue 16 centuries later. In fact, a significant portion of the New Testament letters is given specifically to this problem. Yet, no great church split took place. The council didn't come to a fractured end.

After listening to Peter, who simply related his own personal experience with Gentile Christians, and Barnabas and Paul, who spoke of the wonderful things that God was doing among the "uncircumcised," the recognized leader of the council, James, voiced the group's desire to be in step with what God was doing. They established a foundation of Christian practice that was more than a compromise between the protagonist and antagonists (see vv. 28-29). After spending time in the Scriptures and seeking the guidance of the Holy Spirit through prayer, the council established a principled pattern of both attitude and behavior that still serve the church well. What began as a theological conflict of ideas, ended with a strong, biblically grounded principle of Christian discipleship for individual believers and the church as a whole. The theological controversy regarding the circumcision of Gentile Christians was a good church conflict.

What We Need

I am not naive. Nor am I a blind optimist when it comes to church conflicts. Would that all church conflicts could turn out as well as these two examples from the Early Church. They haven't. Church history is littered with examples of bad church conflicts that have ended in broken churches, broken relationships, broken spirits, and broken bodies. Contemporary churches are contributing new horror stories to the record of brokenness. I've been a part of a few bad church fights myself. It is a tragedy, and a mostly unnecessary one at that.

Imagine what might happen if, when conflicts occur, church members begin to seek the opportunity to clarify and strengthen the central focus and mission of the church or group rather than focusing on personalities or preferences. Imagine what might emerge if, in the midst of conflict, church members begin to pursue the opportunity to find out new information or broadened perspectives rather than stubbornly seeing only their side of the issue. Imagine what might take place if, when conflicts are recognized, church members would think about how relationships and initiatives can grow stronger as a result of working together through the conflicts rather than being preoccupied with "getting our way." Imagine what kind of church might result from church members who gather together to absorb God's word in Scripture and seek God's guidance in prayer before they made important decisions about conflicts rather than dragging out or drudging up the ugly past of our own experience. Just imagine how different the church historical record would be. Imagine how different life might be for Pastor Kelly and her family, John and Mary, Pastor Jones, the Greens, the Brookses, and the congregations they represent.

Disagreements, differences of perspective, and conflicting opinions in the church are inevitable. To be free of these is a sure sign that nothing bad or good is happening. Congregations that intend to accomplish something significant for God cannot be satisfied with homogenous, uniform harmony. What we all need is a *good* church conflict.

Scriptures Cited: Acts 2:44; 6:1-7; 15:1-29; Romans 12:10; Ephesians 4:3, 5; Hebrews 13:17

About the Author: Dr. Ed Robinson is professor of religious education at Nazarene Theological Seminary, Kansas City, Missouri.

CHAPTER 13

CHRISTIAN UNITY

by C. S. COWLES

IN HIS PULITZER PRIZE winning book, *Lives of a Cell*, Lewis Thomas tells us that if we extract and separate a dozen tiny muscle fibers from a fully developed chick's embryo, drop them in a saline solution, and watch them through a microscope, we will see something extraordinary happen. At first, they throb irregularly and chaotically. And then, as if responding to the movement of an invisible conductor's baton, they will begin to pulse in unison.

Something like that occurred on the Jewish feast day of Pentecost, when at the "sound like the blowing of a violent rushing wind" (Acts 2:2), a vast multitude of people, representing at least 16 different language groups, gathered. They were amazed to discover that each heard the apostles speaking news of Christ alive "in his own language" (v. 6). Before the sun set that day, 3,000 strangers had become one body of baptized believers. Those who had little in common now "were together and had everything in common" (v. 44). Surely, this supernaturally created unity is a phenomenon that begs to be explored.

The Unity of the Body

Underneath all that divides the Church—multiplied denominations, diverse doctrinal emphases, differing worship styles, disparate lifestyle standards—there is an invisible but none-the-less real tie that binds all true believers together into "one body in Christ" (Romans 12:5, NASB). This unity, in the midst of such rich diversity, has three vitally important characteristics.

First, it is an *organic unity.* Thirty-one times in his letters Paul describes the church as the Body of Christ. Two examples are Ephesians 5:23 and Romans 12:5. The mystical union between Christ and His visible Body, the Church, is not one attribute among many but constitutes its very essence. The interconnectedness between the invisible Head and the visible Body is not organizational but organic, not physical but spiritual, not external but internal. It is not of human origin but divine. The Church (Greek *ecclesia,* "church," means "called out ones") is called into being by Jesus.

The human body is composed of some 100 trillion cells that constitute an organic whole. Each cell functions as a micro-universe within itself, and yet at the same time perfectly fits in and cooperates with every other cell. Without the sustenance they receive from the whole body, individual cells would quickly perish. The secret is a chemically coiled strand of proteins embedded in each cell, something scientists call DNA. The DNA not only carries instructions directing what each cell should become and do—bone, blood, muscle, tendon, nerve, skin, hair—but each contains the genetic code of the entire human body. All the submicroscopic DNA chains in a person's body could easily fit into an ice cube. Yet if they were unwound and stitched together, the strand would stretch from the earth to the sun and back more than 400 times.

By the indwelling presence of the Holy Spirit, Christ is like DNA in every believer. Nearly 150 times in his letters, Paul uses the expressions "Christ in you" and being "in Christ" to describe this mystical interrelatedness. Jesus' spiritual DNA not only binds all believers to himself in one body but also assigns to each "different kinds of gifts," inspires "different kinds of service," and accomplishes "different kinds of working" (1 Corinthians 12:4-6). "All these [diverse manifestations] are the work of one and the same Spirit" (12:11).

If one part of the Church ignores another part, the organic unity is broken. Paul responds to such an attitude, "The eye cannot say to the hand, 'I don't need you!' And the head cannot say to the feet, 'I don't need you!'" (1 Corinthians 12:21). One theologian rightly observes, "It is not the differences in themselves which are harmful, but only *excluding* and *exclusive* differences. . . . Such differences are divisive and make Church fellowship impossible."[1]

Over against all who would divide the Church, Paul assures us, "You are the body of Christ, and *each one of you is a part of it*" (1 Corinthians 12:27, emphasis added). He also reminds us that what unites us is far more important than what divides us. "You were called to one hope when you were called—one Lord, one faith, one baptism; one God and Father of all, who is over all and through all and in all" (Ephesians 4:4-5). What Jesus says of marriage can also be said of the "tie that binds" believers to Christ and one another. "Therefore what God has joined together, let man not separate" (Mark 10:9).

Second, it is a *confessional unity*. Responding to an exhilarating flash of insight, Peter exclaimed, "You are the Christ, the Son of the living God" (Matthew 16:16). To which Jesus replied, "Blessed are you, Simon son of Jonah, for this was not revealed to you by man, but by my Father in heaven" (16:17). Peter's straightforward confession of faith, unfortunately, is not good enough for some. In a ringing *Call to Evangelical Unity*, a group of prominent evangelical scholars, pastors, and leaders launched a "Doctrinal Renewal Project" in 2000. Their intent was to spell out the essential truth of the gospel around which all evangelicals could unite. It states, in its preamble, that "All Christians are called to unity in love and unity in truth."[2]

There's a catch to their lofty vision, however. In an effort to define precisely what it is that constitutes the "truth" of the gospel, they posit 18 doctrinal affirmations matched with 18 denials, each of which has the effect of cutting off from the Body vast segments of the global church, believers who define the gospel in slightly different terms. One of their affirmations, for instance, virtually excludes all who are committed to the Wesleyan theological tradition. Wesleyans, along with Eastern Orthodox believers and many others, celebrate the incredibly good news that we are not only *declared* to be holy but actually *become* holy through the purifying power of the Holy Spirit who indwells us by faith (see Acts 15:8-9; Romans 6:1-11, 22; 2 Corinthians 5:17; 1 Thessalonians 5:23-24; 1 Peter 1:15-16; 1 John 1:7, 9).

Over against those who would parse the gospel so narrowly as to disqualify as "true Christians" the overwhelming majority of Christians—including Billy Graham, whose most vitriolic critics have come from the ranks of fellow evangelicals—stands the foundational apostolic affirmation. "If you confess with your mouth, 'Jesus is Lord,' and believe in your heart that God raised him from the dead, *you will be saved*" (Romans 10:9, emphasis added). That's it. No qualifications, no exceptions, no exclusions. To his evangelical critics, Billy Graham has one response. "I believe that the Lord called me to preach the Gospel to everybody and to love everybody."[3] John Wesley promoted unity like this, "For opinions, or terms, let us not destroy the work of God. Dost thou love and serve God? It is enough. I give thee the right hand of fellowship."[4]

Third, it is an *intentional unity*. The Early Church demonstrated by the way they made important decisions that they were united in purpose even when they were divided in practice. Both the choosing of the seven in Acts 6:1-7 and the doctrinal meeting at Jerusalem in Acts 15:1-29 are prime examples. Such agreement was neither easy nor automatic, nor did it preclude heated debate over critical doctrinal issues. Rather, their togetherness arose from the realization that what was of ultimate importance was not meticulous observance of Mosaic Law but salvation in Christ. It's not that sound doctrine is unimportant or Christian lifestyle standards inconsequential. Bad theology leads to bad behavior, and bad behavior leads to death. Rather, it was the realization that "God our Savior . . . wants all men to be saved and to come to a knowledge of the truth" (1 Timothy 2:3). After that everything else is, as they say in Idaho, "small potatoes."

The Scandal of the Fractured Body

Though it was a small sidebar item in the news in the summer of 2002, it has vast symbolic significance. A fistfight broke out in Palestine on the roof of the Church of the Holy Sepulcher between Ethiopian and Coptic Christians who had shared custodial responsibilities for generations. It began when a Copt inadvertently placed his chair on the Ethiopian's side of the sepulcher's roof. He claimed that the Ethiopians then poked him and brought some women who came behind him and pinched him. Before the resulting melee was over, 11 monks—7 Ethiopians and 4 Copts—were hospitalized.[5]

That might be considered laughable, but the genocidal fury that swept Rwanda in the spring of 1994 was not. In 100 days, the majority Hutus massacred 800,000 minority Tutsis and Tutsi sympathizers. Since 85 percent of Rwanda's population were baptized Christians, it was another tragic instance, seen too many times in church history, of Christians slaughtering Christians.

As scandalous and as indefensible as are such "[un]holy wars," even these pale in comparison to the less physical but no less destructive schisms, splits, and divisions that have ripped apart the delicate fabric of the visible Body of Christ. While the preceding chapters in this book recognize that conflict is not only inevitable but often necessary, and if handled creatively may strengthen relational bonds, there is no mistaking the fact that conflict can—and often does—divide, damage, and destroy. Conflict carries within itself the seeds of hostility, division, and destruction. Faced with factional rivalries that were tearing apart the church at Corinth, Paul warned, "If anyone destroys God's temple, God will destroy him; for God's temple is sacred, and you are that temple" (1 Corinthians 3:17).

There is scarcely a family or a congregation that does not bear scars of conflicts that have broken up marriages, destroyed homes, split churches, and done untold damage to the cause of Christ. Christians have shown a reprehensible propensity for maligning, attacking, and destroying one another. The blasted and blighted debris of such battles litter the human landscape. And over all this carnage our Lord weeps, for it defeats His desire as expressed in John 17:20-23.

We can feel the heartache as Paul writes the fractious Corinthians, "I *appeal* to you . . . in the name of our Lord Jesus Christ, that all of you agree with one another so that there may be no divisions among you and that you may be *perfectly united* in mind and thought" (1 Corinthians 1:10, emphasis added). While conflict may be a positive force for confronting and resolving important issues, it can also be a telltale sign that the combatants are not "spiritual" but "worldly—mere infants in Christ" (1 Corinthians 3:1). It was no small matter to Paul that two women in the church at Philippi, who had worked along side him "in the cause of the gospel" (Philippians 4:3) would be at odds with each other. That is why he wrote, "I plead with Euodia and I plead with Syntyche to agree with each other in the Lord" (4:2). We should no more justify contentious conflict than we justify sin.

That is why Paul urges us to "make every effort to keep the unity of the Spirit through the bond of peace" (Ephesians 4:3). It is not the "God of war" who sanctifies us "through and through" but the "God of peace" (1 Thessalonians 5:23). The author of Hebrews exhorts us to "make every effort to live in peace with all men and to be holy; without holiness no one will see the Lord" (12:14). We must ceaselessly strive to resolve and overcome all that would divide the Church in a spirit of accepting, forgiving, and reconciling *agape* love.

Cultivating the Fine Art of Peacemaking

In the 12th chapter of his powerful letter to the Romans, Paul offered practical, down-to-earth suggestions as to how we can accomplish peacemaking.

First, *be humble* (12:3). Albert Einstein observed that a little knowledge makes one arrogant, while more knowledge makes one humble. Fortunate is the person who knows enough to know that he or she knows very little. Such a one is less likely to arrogantly superimpose his or her ideas and opinions on others in a contentious way that raises defenses, strains relationships, and increases the likelihood of an explosive confrontation.

Second, *be cooperative* (12:4-8). The difference between cacophony and symphony is the willingness of each musician in an orchestra to play his or her instrument in a way that harmonizes with all the others under the direction of a single conductor. To change the metaphor, a rope with four strands intertwined tightly is not 4 times but 16 times stronger than each strand by itself. We can accomplish in community what we can never achieve separately.

Third, *be loving, forgiving, and kind* (12:9-12). Expressive verbs explode in this paragraph: "love," "cling," "devoted," "honor," "share," "serving." Verbs, as we learned in school, are "action words." These are the "action words" of putting love into practice. Sincere Christians can spend a lifetime doing these things and never exhaust all the possibilities. And how would such active persons have any energy left over for selfish fighting?

Fourth, *be generous* (12:13). The sign of a Spirit-filled church is common people exhibiting uncommon generosity. Such it was on the Day of Pentecost, when "all the believers were together and had everything in common. Selling their possessions and goods, they gave to anyone as he had need" (Acts 2:44-45). The work of Christ through His visible Body, the Church, would be immeasurably crippled were it not for the steady, faithful, and sacrificial giving of its members. Mother Teresa, for instance, took the half-million dollars she received with the Nobel Peace Prize and invested it all in building new homes for several thousand of Calcutta's homeless families.

Fifth, *be a peacemaker* (12:14-20). The problem with heated conflict situations is that they bring out the worst traits in the combatants. A good warning to remember is, "Be careful that in fighting monsters you do not become a monster." That is why Paul wrote, "As far as it depends on you, live at peace with everyone. . . . Do not be overcome by evil, but overcome evil with good" (12:18, 21). Paul's own actions matched his words. "When we are cursed, we bless; when we are persecuted, we endure it; when we are slandered, we answer kindly" (1 Corinthians 4:12-13).

Conclusion

It was a worship service never to be forgotten. The newly elected general superintendent, presiding over our district assembly for the first time, came down in front of the altar before preaching to an overflow evening crowd. "There's a dear brother in this congregation," he began, "with whom I have had a strained relationship in the past. We were forced into positions, not of our own choosing, that threw us into an unfortunate conflict situation that extended far too long and involved far too many people."

Moving down the aisle, he addressed the "brother" directly. "I want to seek your forgiveness for anything I may have said or done that needlessly hurt you. I'm sorry." Before he could even finish his apology, the lay leader to whom he was speaking got out of his seat and moved into the aisle, where they fell into each other's arms weeping. To say that heaven came down and glory filled that church that evening would be a vast understatement.

For many years, I have carried this prayer in the flyleaf of my Bible:

O Lord, make me the instrument of thy peace.
  Where there is hatred, let me sow love;
  Where there is injury, pardon;
  Where there is discord, union;
  Where there is doubt, faith;
  Where there is despair, hope;
  Where there is darkness, light;
  Where there is sadness, joy;
O Lord, grant that we seek
  Not to be consoled but to console;
  Not to be understood, but to understand;
  Not to be loved, but to love.
For it is in giving that we receive,
  In forgetting that we find ourselves,
  In pardoning that we are pardoned,
  And in dying that we are born to eternal life. Amen.[6]

Such a beautiful prayer promotes Christian unity. May we find it real in our lives.

Notes:

1. Hans Küng, *The Church* (New York: Sheed and Ward, 1967), 276.

2. "A Call to Evangelical Unity," *Christianity Today,* June 14, 1999, special supplement.

3. *The San Diego Union-Tribune,* Sunday, May 4, 2003, Special section, "Billy Graham Mission: San Diego," 3.

4. *The Complete Works of John Wesley,* vol. 8 (Albany, Oreg.: AGES Software, 1997), 408.

5. <www.mediaethiopia.com/August102.htm>

6. Attributed to Francis of Assisi.

Scriptures Cited: Matthew 16:16-17; Mark 10:9; John 17:20-23; Acts 2:2, 6, 44; 6:1-7; 15:1-29; Romans 6:1-11, 22; 10:9; 12:1-21; 1 Corinthians 1:10; 3:1, 17; 4:12-13; 12:4-6, 11, 21, 27; 2 Corinthians 5:17; Ephesians 4:3-5; 5:23; Philippians 4:2-3; 1 Thessalonians 5:23-24; 1 Timothy 2:3; Hebrews 12:14; 1 Peter 1:15-16; 1 John 1:7, 9

About the Author: Dr. C. S. Cowles is professor of philosophy and religion at Point Loma Nazarene University, San Diego, California.